THE STRANGER WHO BORE ME

Adoptee–Birth Mother Relationships

The issue of adoptees making contact with their birth parents is often a contentious one. The traditional practice of denying adoptees knowledge of their genetic parents creates a very distinct social reality for the adoptees; secrecy sets them apart as a separate category of people with suspect family membership and questionable social identity. Karen March examines how some adoptees make contact with their birth mother to manage their ambiguous social status.

In *The Stranger Who Bore Me* sixty adult adoptees discuss the difficulties they have encountered in a world where biological kinship governs. Each of their stories reveals the personal dilemma created by the societal demand for secrecy and the deep pain and intense joy associated with adoptees making contact with their birth mother. Karen March has created a compelling and informative analysis of this need of some adoptees.

Little research has been done on the actual outcome of adoptee–birth parent reunion and most arguments in this controversial area are based on personal anecdotal reports. This book offers the first systematic study of the consequences of reunion. As such it is an invaluable guide for any member of an adoptive triad as well as for professionals and government officials in the field of adoption.

Any adoptee, adoptive parent, or birth parent may be faced with the reality of contact. The stories told in this book will help them cope with that event and provide others with the knowledge and insight needed to understand and support those who initiated it.

KAREN MARCH is a member of the Department of Sociology and Anthropology, Carleton University.

KAREN MARCH

The Stranger Who Bore Me: Adoptee–Birth Mother Relationships

UNIVERSITY OF TORONTO PRESS
Toronto Buffalo London

60110732

© University of Toronto Press Incorporated 1995
Toronto Buffalo London
Printed in Canada

ISBN 0-8020-0447-4 (cloth)
ISBN 0-8020-7235-6 (paper)

Printed on acid-free paper

Canadian Cataloguing in Publication Data

March, Karen Ruth
  The stranger who bore me : adoptee–birth mother relationships

  Includes bibliographical references and index.
  ISBN 0-8020-0447-4 (bound)   ISBN 0-8020-7235-6 (pbk.)

  1. Adoptees.   2. Adoptees – Psychology.
  3. Birth mothers.   4. Mother and child.   5. Adoption –
  Canada.   I. Title

  HV875.M37 1995   362.82'98   C94-932735-2

University of Toronto Press acknowledges the financial assistance to its publishing
program of the Canada Council and the Ontario Arts Council.

This book has been published with the help of a grant from the Social Science
Federation of Canada, using funds provided by the Social Sciences and Humanities
Research Council of Canada.

In memory of my parents
Carl Lewis Avey
and
Mary Elmira Haines

Contents

viii   Contents

Tables

Preface

The institution of adoption in Canada was founded on the belief that a successful outcome of adoption requires concealment of the adopted child's biological family background. This practice of non-disclosure creates a very different social reality for adoptees, however, than intended originally. By denying adoptees access to both the genetic and genealogical information possessed by the majority of their society, secrecy distinguishes them as a separate category of people with suspect family membership and questionable social identity. This book examines how some adoptees use contact with their birth mothers to manage that social status.

The sixty reunited adoptees who appear in this book discuss the difficulties encountered by people who lack genealogical and genetic heritage in a world where biological kinship governs. They describe how this missing information affected their presentation of self, their increasing desire for more complete biological backgrounds, and their need to establish contact with their birth mothers. Individually, each of these stories reveals the personal dilemmas created by the demand for secrecy in adoption. Together, these journeys into the unknown territory of contact with birth mothers present a compelling and informative analysis of the human capacity for self-awareness. As such, the accounts in this book provide a strong appreciation of the need for some adoptees to establish a relationship denounced by their society.

Adoptees' contact with birth mothers contests the institution of adoption as it now exists in Canada. However, this book engages in that debate in a very limited way. Contact with birth mothers is a reality. Political lobby groups are succeeding in their demand for open record systems, in which all members of the adoption triangle – adoptees, birth parents, and adoptive parents – may obtain identifying information on the others. Any adoptee, adoptive parent, or birth parent may be faced with the possibility of contact whether he or she wishes it or not. I hope that the stories offered in this book will help in coping with that event. I hope also that these stories will provide others with the sensitivity needed to understand and support those engaged in this contact.

In line with this objective, this book presents, as much as possible, the process of the search for and contact with the birth mother (and father) in the adoptees' own words. Chapter 1 sets the stage for that discussion with a brief overview of the issues surrounding secrecy in adoption. Chapter 2 summarizes the methodology used in collection of the data for this study. The five chapters that follow consider the search process and the results of contact with birth mothers. Chapter 3 describes the initial period of introspection involved in the decision to search and the events leading to initiation of the search. Chapter 4 outlines the search process. The decision to contact the birth mother, the types of approaches to contact, and the outcomes of contact appear in Chapter 5. Chapter 6 examines the patterns of interaction between birth mothers and adoptees. Satisfaction with the search and birth mother are examined in Chapter 7. All these chapters explore the implications of secrecy for the social construction of reality and the effects of secrecy on adoptees who desire contact with their birth mothers.

Acknowledgments

The people who appear in this book have taken risks with self that few of us would venture to take. I am grateful for having been allowed by them to participate in their lives.

Others have influenced my work, as well. My mentor, Ralph Matthews, ensured this publication through his constant faith in my ability to 'do good.' Engaging questions offered by Billy Shaffir and Jim Rice sharpened my analysis. David Magder counselled me gently through the private thoughts and images evoked by my research experiences. As a 'gatekeeper,' Marie Louise Kuttschrutter helped me gain the understanding needed to cope with many of the barriers between myself and adoptees who desire contact with their birth mothers. Rhoda Howard's unfailing support, both as an academic and as a friend, encouraged me during some of my greatest periods of self-doubt. My close friends, Gail Coulas, David Lewis, and Linda Muzzin provided invaluable 'reflected appraisals' which inspired my self-confidence. This acknowledgment is inadequate compensation for the personal and professional gifts given to me by these people.

My family, Art, David, and Stephen, deserve considerable credit for standing by me throughout the endless days and nights that I gave to this study instead of to them. I can only guess at the sacrifices they endured. I can never thank them enough.

THE STRANGER WHO BORE ME

1

Adoption, Secrecy, and the Desire for Reunion

The legalization of non-disclosure in adoption places severe restrictions on the release of information involving members of the adoption triad. In particular, the original birth records are sealed and adoptees are denied access to information on their biological family background. Large numbers of adoptees claim that their missing genetic and genealogical background inhibits their development of a coherent identity structure. Many of those adoptees have searched for, and achieved contact with, their birth mothers who provide them with this background information. Their decision to go against the laws of their society has led to a series of studies on the motivation for this search and the outcomes of this contact. These studies reveal positive identity effects for adoptees who successfully merge their newly discovered biological background information as a part of self. In preparation for a more complete understanding of this process of search and contact, this chapter describes the perceived need secrecy in adoption and the findings produced by other research studies.

PERCEIVED NEED FOR SECRECY IN ADOPTION

All societies practise adoption in some form. Simple preliterate societies often 'give' children to other kin members who may need extra help or who have more resources to successfully raise those children to adulthood. In such societies, adoption is an informal, open arrangement in which adopted children possess full knowledge of their birth parents' identity and maintain contact with their original kinship group (Kirk, 1981: 3). In a modern, industrialized society like Canada, however, increased residential mobility, technological innovation, and corporate capitalism have decreased the power and scope of extended kinship ties. Here, adoption has become an institutionalized structure concerned mainly with matching childless couples with children who need parental care (Benet, 1976: 14). State agents mediate the transfer of those children from their biological families to their new adoptive parents. A contractual agreement of non-disclosure supports that transfer by sealing all identifying information on the adopted child's genealogical and genetic background (Garber, 1985).

During the 1920s, when adoption was legalized formally in the various provinces in Canada, secrecy was viewed as a safeguard for the interests of all members in the adoption triangle – the adoptee, the birth parents, and the adoptive parents (Garber, 1985: 13–15). By eliminating the likelihood of the future intrusion of the birth parents into the adoptee's life, secrecy ensured adoptive parents' exclusive custody over their adopted children. In addition, secrecy protected the confidentiality of birth parents who experienced social stigma from relinquishing their illegitimate children to others. Secrecy sheltered adoptees also from openly confronting the questionable moral background of birth parents who had conceived them under 'suspicious' circumstances (Benet, 1976: 12–14).

Yet, by denying adoptees access to their genealogical and genetic backgrounds, secrecy produces an unexpected side-effect for adopted children. Unlike children raised within their biological families, adopted children possess two different sets of parents who fulfil separate functions. Adoptive parents perform the parental role. This set of parents provides adoptees with a family structure, socializes them as members of their society, and raises them into adulthood. Birth parents provide a genealogical and genetic heritage. This set of parents gives adoptees their physical traits, emotional temperaments, and intellectual abilities. However, by sealing adopted children's original birth records, non-disclosure denies adoptees access to the source of their genetic traits. It denies them knowledge of the role played by the birth parents in their development as human beings.

It was not until the first cohort of adopted children reached adulthood that the problematic relationship between non-disclosure and the division of parental functions became apparent (Clothier, 1943; Dukette, 1962; Lemon, 1959; Sants, 1965; Schecter et al., 1964; Toussieng, 1962). Many adoptees began to express discomfort over their lack of access to information on their biological backgrounds, and they requested contact with their birth parents. These requests presented particular problems when applied retroactively to birth parents and adoptive parents who had been promised and had expected lifetime anonymity (Sweeney, 1986: 15). Given the strong public support for non-disclosure, adoptees' requests were denied in favour of the status quo.

Many adoptees were not satisfied with this definition of the situation, and they continued their demands for complete biological backgrounds. Their actions have raised public interest in the issue of the need for secrecy in adoption versus the 'need to know'. That public interest is fostered by the concentrated efforts of self-help search groups campaigning actively for reform of adoption law. Because the membership of these groups views reunion as a natural outgrowth of an adoption system based on non-disclosure, they work especially hard on establishing open record systems that would allow all members of the adoption triangle access to identifying information. This identifying information could then be used to establish contact with the other members. For an analysis of the open records debate in Canada, see Garber (1985) or Sachdev (1989).

SELF-HELP SEARCH ORGANIZATIONS AND THEIR IMPACT

The development of self-help search groups began in 1954 when Jean Paton published *The Adopted Break Silence*. Paton had interviewed forty adult adoptees about their perception of their adoptive experience. Although very satisfied with the outcome of their adoption, these adoptees reported confusion over their different biological and sociocultural heritages. They expressed frustration over the demands of secrecy and their inability to synthesize their two separate backgrounds into some type of unified whole. Their reports supported Paton's view as an adoptee who questioned her own biological origins. The interest shown by other adoptees who read Paton's book and also desired contact with their birth mothers led her to create Orphan Voyage, the first, formal, self-help organization to support adoptees with their search for their birth mothers.

In 1973, Florence Fisher further advanced the idea of contact with birth mothers when she published the story of her twenty-year search for her birth parents (Fisher, 1973). Like Paton, Fisher created a self-help search organization in response to the positive reactions to her book. Fisher became more politically active than Paton, however, and her organization, the Adoptee's Liberty Movement Association (ALMA) strongly lobbied for adoption law reform. The publicity gained from ALMA's political activities has led to a stronger awareness of adoptees' desire for contact and has legitimated their search actions.

ALMA and Orphan Voyage are now the largest national adoptee groups in the United States – with many branch organizations extending across that country. The publicity stimulated by their members' search and reunion activities has given rise to numerous splinter groups designed to address the particular interests of adoptees, birth parents, and adoptive parents: for example, Yesterday's Children, Concerned United Birthparents (CUB), the Adoption Identity Movement (AIM), and Adoptive Parents for Open Records (APFOR). In the United Kingdom, the National Organization for Reunion of Child and Parent (NORCAP) and Contact are the two major search groups. Australia houses the head office of Jigsaw International, while New Zealand supports its branch offices. Such self-help search organizations have given all members of the adoption triangle the emotional, social, and political support needed to demand open record systems. The creative search techniques used by their members have helped other searchers bypass many of the legal constraints imposed by non-disclosure. In this way, large numbers of searching adoptees have achieved contact without their society's formal approval or legal consent. Their success has, in turn, forced social service agencies and legislators to address the issue of open record systems in adoption.

The largest self-help search group in Canada is Parent Finders. Like other self-help search groups, Parent Finders extends emotional assistance during search, offers knowledge of successful searching techniques, and helps individual members through the various stages of search and contact. With branch offices in each province, Parent Finders provides intermediaries who counsel individual members on their expectations of contact and facilitates contacts with birth mothers. The political activism of Parent Finders has been very effective in the implementation of several voluntary reunion registries across Canada (Sachdev, 1989: 2).

Self-help search organizations plead their case for contact with birth mothers as a human rights issue (Griffith, 1991). While adoption gives adoptees a new set of parents whom they love and respect, secrecy repudiates the existence of their birth parents (Flynn, 1979: 3). As such, non-disclosure denies adoptees' inherited traits at the same time that it casts doubt over the source of their uninherited characteristics (Harrington, 1980: 37). By outlining the contribution of their birth parents to their development as human beings, reunion helps adoptees sort out these inconsistencies. Until an open record system is enacted fully in adoption, adoptees are denied vital information about themselves that other members of their society readily possess.

NON-DISCLOSURE AND IDENTITY

Researchers have responded to the noticeable number of adoptees requesting contact with their birth mothers. In the first comprehensive study conducted on search and reunion, Triseliotis (1973) interviewed seventy adult adoptees who obtained access to their original birth certificates through the open record system established in Scotland. Despite his initial belief in reunion as a symptom of negative adoption outcome or individual pathology, Triseliotis found neither vindictiveness nor poor adoptive parent–child relationships among his sample. He decided that searching behaviour emerged mainly from the adoptee's desire for more self-knowledge and self-understanding. Thus, Triseliotis (1973: 157) concluded that, as long as secrecy prevailed in adoption, adoptees would demonstrate some preoccupation with their origins and the identity of their unknown biological parents.

Sorosky et al. (1974, 1975, 1978) reported similar results in their studies of searching American adoptees. Their research sample described identity 'gaps' created by the adoptees' inability to provide an adequate account of their biological background to themselves or others (1974: 204). Adoptees saw their search as a way to 'fill in those gaps' by meeting with the unknown biological parents who possessed that information. Therefore, Sorosky et al. (1974: 205) advised a reconsideration of 'the degree to which an adoptee is able to resolve questions about his or her identity without having more complete information on the birth parents and without the opportunity of a reunion.'

Subsequent research studies confirm this intense need of some adoptees to complete their identity through reunion (Anderson, 1989: 625; Gonyo and Watson, 1988; Haimes and Timms, 1985; Pacheco and Eme, 1993; Sachdev, 1992; Simpson et al., 1981; Sobol and Cardiff, 1983; Stoneman et al., 1980; Thompson et al., 1978). Like Triseliotis and Sorosky et al., these researchers report high levels of emotional stability and personal adjustment among searching adoptees (Norvell and Guy, 1977: 445; Day, 1979). Searchers demonstrate little dissatisfaction with their adoptive parents or with the outcome of their adoption and little difficulty attaining their goals or objectives in life (Haimes and Timms, 1985: 51; Pacheco and Eme, 1993: 58). Adoptees' searching activity stems mainly from their desire to complete their identity through knowledge of their missing genealogical and genetic backgrounds.

These search and reunion studies reveal no specific sociological category or personality type that will help determine which adoptees will most likely search, which will engage in reunion contact, or which will report a successful outcome of contact with the birth mother (Haimes and Timms, 1985: 51; Sachdev, 1992: 58). Adoption appears as the only clearly identifiable variable to consolidate searching adoptees into a distinctly unified group (Pacheco and Eme, 1993: 58; Sorosky et al., 1978). This sole unifying factor of adoption is understandable, however, because it is the legal requirement for non-disclosure in adoption that denies searching adoptees access to their background information.

Follow-up studies on outcomes of reunions support the reported links between secrecy and the need for identity completion through contact with the birth mother. Reunited adoptees report a deeper sense of personal cohesion and unity from the genealogical knowledge gained through contact with birth relatives (Simpson et al., 1981: 432). They describe themselves as more content with themselves, more self-confident, more satisfied with their lives, more tolerant of other people, more mature in their outlook, and more at peace and settled within themselves after having access to their genealogical and genetic information (Stoneman et al., 1980: 14; Thompson et al., 1978: 14). This sense of completion of identity occurs also for adoptees who contact birth relatives where the birth mother has died before the search was completed. Although disappointed not to meet with the birth mother, they find that contact with birth relatives 'eases their pain of wondering' (Sachdev, 1992: 65) by removing their doubts about their biological background.

Search and reunion studies provide a firm foundation for an examination of the relationship between the need of searching adoptees' for more genealogical information and their desire for reunion. They offer a limited analysis of the outcome of the contact, however, because of the small number of reunions actually explored. For example, of the seventy adoptees in Triseliotis's (1973) study, only eleven experienced reunion. During their examination of 133 searching adoptees in Toronto, Thompson et al. (1978) encountered a similar pattern – 11 adoptees achieved reunion. Simpson et al. (1981: 427) found twelve reunited adoptees in their study of '41 genetic searches initiated and completed by a public agency between June 1977 and December 1978' in the United States. Stoneman et al. (1980) gained a volunteer sample of only twenty reunited adoptees for their Canadian study on outcome of reunion for all three members of the adoption triangle. Depp (1982) sent letters and questionnaires on search and outcome of reunion to twelve reunited adoptees in Virginia and received only ten responses. These small samples restrict the generalizability of reported reunion results to the larger population of adoptees considering search and reunion (Sachdev, 1989: 18).

The majority of the adoptees in these search and reunion studies represent volunteer subjects who have sought reunion mainly through social service agencies or government reunion registries (Haimes and Timms, 1985; Simpson et al., 1981; Sobol and Cardiff, 1983; Sorosky et al., 1974; 1975; 1978;

Stoneman et al., 1980; Thompson et al., 1978). Because self-help search organizations facilitate a large number of adoptee–birth mother contacts, the positive contact experiences reported in those studies may be influenced by the professional counselling services provided by such agencies. Many of these searchers report independent search attempts before they contacted the social service agency for assistance (Simpson et al., 1981: 482; Sorosky et al., 1974: 198; Triseliotis, 1973: 6). Thus, these samples of searching adoptees may represent those adoptees who initially experience difficult or unsuccessful self-help search attempts. The bulk of searching adoptees gain reunion through self-help search organizations, and the search and contact experiences reported in those studies may, therefore, be atypical.

To counteract the inadequacies appearing in this research literature, Gonyo and Watson (1988) examined the information records on registration calls made by 488 adoptees to an adoption search support group and by thirty-one adoptees to a child welfare agency reunion registry in Chicago, Illinois, during the years 1985 and 1986. These researchers found similar demographic characteristics and search concerns between both groups of adoptees and the reports of previous research samples. Although this large sample of support group searchers removed doubt over possible differences between the two types of search populations, Gonyo and Watson lacked details on the outcome of reunion because their analysis was based mainly on intake data.

Sachdev (1992) has completed a study of 124 Anglo-Saxon adoptees who achieved reunion through Parent Finders in Ontario. He sent structured questionnaires to the organization's reunited adoptee members asking them to complete and return the questionnaires to him with their comments. These reunited adoptees resembled the samples found in previous studies. Like other reunited adoptees, they reported a more cohesive identity from 'the experience of being able to connect themselves for the first time with their generational line and to share physical resemblances and interests with someone related by blood' (Sachdev, 1992: 64). Like other reunited adoptees, they believed that knowledge of their genealogical background helped them accept their present condition and circumstances with greater equanimity. Ninety-nine per cent claimed 'no regrets' about the outcome of their search contact (Sachdev, 1992: 55).

Pacheco and Eme (1993) found similar patterns of identity cohesion in their examination of a randomly selected sample of seventy-two reunited adoptees who were members of a Chicago adoption reunion support group. These adoptees completed a telephone interview based on a structured questionnaire designed to gain responses on satisfaction with the outcome of contact. Their search and contact experiences closely matched Sachdev's find-ings, with 87 per cent reporting that they were very highly or moderately pleased with their outcome and 94 per cent having 'no regrets' (Pacheco and Eme, 1993: 60). Pacheco and Eme concluded, therefore, that 'the main source of such general positive experiences would seem to be that even in those cases in which the experience proved to be negative, the feeling that the 'puzzle is solved' is the bottom line.

GENEALOGICAL AND GENETIC BACKGROUND, AWARENESS CONTEXTS, AND
ADOPTIVE IDENTITY

This body of literature presents the desire for reunion as an identity issue. Searching adoptees experience identity 'gaps' from their missing genealogical background and their lack of knowledge about the events surrounding their conception, birth, and relinquishment (Haimes and Timms, 1985: 50). Con-tact with their birth mothers provides them with a sense of personal unity and increased self-confidence because it lets them 'sort out' their birth par-ents' contribution to their development as human beings (Sorosky et al., 1974: 203). This body of literature is vague, however, about how this ge-nealogical and genetic knowledge contributes to identity or the way in which it affects the adoptee's view of self. In contrast, the study reported here considers those issues in its examination of the search and contact expe-riences of sixty adult adoptees.

The awareness context paradigm developed by Glazer and Strauss (1967b) serves here as a key component for the analysis of contact with birth mothers. By focusing on the social-structural context within which interaction occurs, the awareness context paradigm studies the interplay between social structure and personal experience and considers how the institutionalization of secrecy in adoption creates a structural situation that affects the daily lives of adop-tees. It outlines the social dilemma encountered by adoptees who, unaware of their genealogical and genetic background, must interact with others who possess ready access to such knowledge about themselves. It reveals, also, how a transformation of the interactional situation through contact with the birth mother may alter the institution of adoption. The demand by searching adoptees for more openness in the adoption process and the right to contact with the birth mother alters the perception of non-disclosure and the need for continued severance of the adopted child's biological kinship ties.

According to Glaser and Strauss (1967b: 430), an awareness context is 'the total combination of what each interactant in a situation knows about the identity of the other and his own identity in the eyes of the other'. *Four* awareness contexts affect the social interaction process: 'An open aware-ness context obtains when each interactant is aware of the other's true iden-tity and his own identity in the eyes of the other. A closed awareness context obtains when an interactant does not know the other's identity or the other's view of his identity. A suspicion awareness context is a modification of the closed one: one interactant suspects the true identity of the other or the other's view of his identity or both. A pretence awareness context is a mod-ification of an open one: both interactants are fully aware but pretend not to be' (Ibid.). One of these four awareness contexts surrounds every social interaction. Adoptees experience closed awareness contexts, for example, during interactions involving disclosure of their genealogical backgrounds or the events surrounding their conception, birth, and relinquishment. That awareness context may transform into a suspicion context when they, or others, guess about the adoptees' ethnic heritage, the birth mother's moral character, or the events leading to the adoption. Some adoptees try to avoid these types of interactional situations by participating in mutual pretence awareness contexts in which they offer, and others accept, the adoptive fam-ily's genealogical background as their own. Adoptees may achieve open awareness contexts, however, only when they gain complete knowledge of their genealogical and genetic backgrounds through contact with the birth mother.

The demand for non-disclosure in adoption limits the ability of individual adoptees to bring their full identity to the social interaction process. It en-velops them within a closed awareness context when such topics as family history, genetic traits, or ethnic background arise. At such times, others may question the adoptees' presentation of self and discriminate against them for being someone other than who they appear to be. This structural situation is offered, in this book, as the major motive for contact with the birth mother. It explains the wide variety of adoptees who search, the lack of a common variable among searchers other than their adoptive status, and the large number of adoptees who express little need for contact with their birth mother (Pacheco and Eme, 1993). Because the open awareness context gained through contact with the birth mother presents one among many management techniques used by adoptees to counteract the effects of non-disclosure, this motive also explains the large numbers of adoptees who may not desire to search or achieve contact with their birth mothers.

Several structural conditions support the closed awareness context pro-duced by non-disclosure. For example, when the adoption is legalized, adop-tees are given a 'false' birth certificate presenting them as biological members of the adoptive family, and their original birth records are sealed (Andrews, 1979). Adoptive parents are advised to treat their adoptive children 'as if born' to that family and to present the adoptive family's genealogy as the adoptee's own (that is, to give the adoptee a false biography).

Others engage in collusive games or pretence awareness contexts that protect those beliefs. They offer a 'chosen child' story in which adoptive parents select that particular child to be a member of their family. They maintain the 'fallen woman' image of the birth mother who, through her own indiscretion, caused her child's relinquishment. They label searching adoptees as deviant, perverse, or psycho-pathological (Haimes and Timms, 1985: 50).

Of particular note are the sociopolitical arguments used to justify the legal implementation of secrecy in adoption. These arguments incorporate three main themes. First, non-disclosure protects the primacy of the adoptive parent–child bond. Birth mother contact, thus, is a betrayal of the adoptive parents' love and affection. Second, non-disclosure protects the birth mother's privacy. Birth mother contact is an intrusion, therefore, into the birth mother's life. Third, non-disclosure protects adoptees from disagreeable knowledge about their birth parents' morality. Thus, contact with the birth mother elicits a dubious relationship with a woman who has a questionable character.

Each of the above structural conditions contributes to the interactional difficulties experienced by adoptees when the topic of genealogical and ge-netic background arises during social interaction. Each is considered, there-fore, by adoptees as they make their search decision, initiate contact with their birth mothers, and try to establish an adoptee–birth mother relation-ship. Thus, three main themes used to support non-disclosure affect the adoptees' perception of the search, the contact with their birth mothers and the outcome of that contact.

The lobbying activities of self-help search organizations have raised con-siderable public interest in the issue of contact with birth mothers. Varying opinions exist on the debate over the implementation of open record systems that negate non-disclosure. That debate masks the reality of the increasing numbers of searching adoptees who bypass the present legal restrictions against reunion and establish contact with their birth mothers.

In response to that reality researchers have examined the search and con-tact process. Studies describe the adoptees' desire for contact with the birth mother as a need for a more cohesive identity. Searching adoptees claim to 'have a piece missing' because they lack complete genealogical and genetic backgrounds and cannot establish their birth parents' contribution to their development as human beings. Contact with their birth mothers creates a more coherent identity structure by letting adoptees merge their genealogical backgrounds with their identities as adult adoptees. These studies do not consider fully the social position of adoptees who live within a social world that uses genetic inheritance and biological kinship to assess family membership and social identity. By creating a closed awareness context around the biological backgrounds of adoptees, non-disclosure places them at a social disadvantage whenever such subjects as family ties, physical appearance, or creative talents arise. It limits adoptees' presentation of self because it limits their knowledge about their birth identity. Contact with their birth mothers changes that closed awareness context into an open awareness context in which adoptees may negotiate equally with others who bring their full identities to the process of social interaction. This is the major motivation for search and the principal factor of consideration for outcome of contact.

The sixty reunited adoptees who were interviewed for this study believed that adoption had separated them from the majority of their society. Repeated encounters with the responses of others to their adoptive status reinforced that belief. Because the responses of others focused on the adoptees original kinship ties and the dubious events surrounding their conception, birth, and relinquishment, these adoptees viewed their missing genealogical and genetic backgrounds as the reason for the social discrimination enacted against them. They saw themselves as more socially acceptable to others after they had gained access to this information, and their reported satisfaction with the outcome of their contact supports that view.

Given this scenario, the prime motivation for reunion lies in the searching adoptees' perception of their adoptive status and the centrality of obtaining information on their biological background to a satisfactory presentation of self. This motivation for the search clarifies the relationship between non-disclosure and fragmentation of identity. It explains the diverse social, emotional, and psychological characteristics of searchers and the wide variation in the interest in contact with the birth mother demonstrated by the adoptee population. It accounts for the inconsistent reports between satisfaction with reunion and the type of genealogical information found or the contact obtained with the birth mother. That motivation emerges as the stories of the search for and contact with the birth mother become revealed in the following chapters of this study.

The data analysis for this research study results mainly from in-depth interviews. This qualitative approach compares with the more structured interview schedules used on larger randomly selected samples of reunited adoptees found in the research literature (Pacheco and Eme, 1993; Sachdev, 1989; 1992). The issues involved in that approach and the methodology used in this research project appear, therefore, in the next chapter.

2

Methodological Issues Involved in the Study of Contact with Birth Mothers

This study describes the search for and contact with the birth mother from the perspective of adoptees who engage in these activities. Such description involves methodologies that focus on the research participants' subjective reality. This chapter summarizes those research procedures. It outlines the way in which this researcher gained a sensitivity towards adoptees' need for contact with their birth mothers; how I tried to use a sympathetic understanding to construct a semi-structured interview questionnaire; how I gained access to a random sample of sixty reunited adoptees as interview subjects; that sample's response to my interview solicitation; and its representativeness as a research sample.

The search and contact research literature exhibits a number of methodological limitations that seem to be inherent in the study of search and contact outcome. This study, too, contains some of those methodological flaws. Consideration of those flaws occurs in this chapter mainly when the flaws bring into question the validity and reliability of this research data. I believe that the sensitivity gained through participant observation sessions with searching and newly reunited adoptees neutralizes many of those concerns.

SENSITIZING ONESELF TO THE RESEARCH TOPIC

The data analysis in this book concentrates more on the subjective meaning of human behaviour than on its objective cause or purpose. This type of research focus requires a 'sympathetic understanding' of the research participants' social experience. That sympathetic understanding develops when researchers 'immerse' themselves in their research participants' social world (Blumer, 1969: 16; Lofland, 1971: 13). Immersion requires researchers to do everything possible 'to get close to that life and know what is going on in it' (Blumer, 1969: 38).

Given this methodological stance, I used every available opportunity to learn about the search for and contact with birth mothers. I began with an intensive investigation of past research studies (Andrews, 1979; Garber, 1985; Haimes and Timms, 1985; Lemon, 1959; McWhinnie, 1967; Simpson et al., 1981; Sobol and Cardiff, 1983; Sorosky et al., 1974; 1975; 1978). I learned that this was a topic of public concern, and I attended Legislative Committee meetings on proposed revisions to the non-disclosure clause contained in the Ontario Child Welfare Act of 1978; I watched television programs and studied all magazine or newspaper articles that I could find on the subject; and I read autobiographical accounts written by reunited adoptees (Fisher, 1973; Marcus, 1981; McKluen, 1978; Paton, 1954; Redmond and Sleightholm, 1982).

To maximize my understanding of the process of the search for and contact with birth mothers as a private issue, I conducted a fifteen-month period of participant observation with two self-help search groups. During that observation period, I followed two adoptees through their search process, accompanied one adoptee to her first contact with her birth mother, and observed three contact calls to birth relatives. I went to a support group meeting of reunited birth mothers and attended a Children's Aid Society panel discussion on search and reunion. These types of research experiences sensitized me to the social reality of the people actually engaged in the process of searching for and contacting birth mothers. Gaining a sympathetic understanding to search and contact required a more intimate association with my research subjects, however, than provided by such isolated incidents. It required continuous interaction with searching and reunited adoptees. I achieved that interaction through participant observation sessions at Parent Finders meetings.

DEVELOPING UNDERSTANDING THROUGH PARTICIPANT OBSERVATION

Because this study is based on the belief that individuals construct or build their own reality from the tools that their social world provides, the researcher must investigate how that reality is constructed and negotiated by the individuals involved. This methodological approach requires that the research participants be given every possible opportunity to provide their own accounts of their social behaviour and their perspective of the social environment in which they exist (Blumer, 1969; Williamson et al., 1977). That research goal achieved through intimate contact with the research participants within their own social environment. This is the only way that data analysis and theory construction can remain constant with the reality of the individuals who experience that reality (Glaser and Strauss, 1967). Participant observation provides this type of intimate contact.

Participant observation is a process of *discovery* in which the researcher acts as a neophyte who learns the meanings that constitute the subject's own social world. In this approach, the researcher becomes an observational member of the group that he or she investigates. He or she commits himself or herself to attending that group for a considerable period of time (i.e., months or years) so he or she can learn and understand the group's frame of reference. Typically, the researcher adopts the separate role of 'observer' and participates only slightly with the group so he or she will not disrupt or influence the group's dynamics. That position demands an open attitude of acceptance towards group rules and group members' behaviour. It also requires a vigilant attitude towards confidentiality and a protection of the research participants' privacy and personal integrity.

The participant observation field literature outlines several problems encountered in 'entering the field,' 'gaining access through brokers,' and 'developing trust and rapport' (Douglas, 1976; Shaffir et al., 1980). I found little difficulty in those areas during the initial stages of this research project. The two self-help search groups chosen for study were members of the larger Canadian self-help search organization known as Parent Finders. Parent Finders holds monthly meetings that are open to the public. Nonmembers attend meetings frequently. The organization also sends group members to engage in panel discussions or public presentations on adoption, search, and contact with the birth mother. Thus, when I contacted both groups to discuss my research project, I was told to 'just come, mingle with the members and see what happens' (Fieldnotes, 12 March 1984: 1; 18 March 1984: 1). When I arrived at my first meeting I found that most group members accepted my presence. I therefore attended meetings with both groups for a fifteen-month period between 1 April 1984 and 31 July 1985. Over this period I observed numerous adoptees engaged in the process of search and early contact with the birth mother.

Parent Finders guarantees its members confidentiality. Group leaders state often during meetings that 'everything that is said in this room stays in this room' (Fieldnotes, 5 August 1984: 2). Members use first names only and rarely ask for personal information unrelated to adoption, search, or contact with the birth mother. I assumed this approach. Whenever possible, I stressed my own belief in confidentiality and my professional ethics as a researcher. In this way, trust and rapport developed between myself, as a researcher, and Parent Finders members, as participants in the research. The following dialogue represents the type of response that occurred when my research practices were questioned,

Adoptee: I feel uncomfortable about this. Perhaps, it's because I'm thinking, 'Why is she asking me all of these questions? Is everything I say going to appear in print somewhere?'

Researcher: That's a reasonable assumption. But, even if what you said was going to be included in my study, it would all be completely confidential. If you want me to omit anything, you can just let me know. I can't even include you if you don't want me to. If you tell me that you don't want me to include you in my fieldnotes, then, I would respect your wishes. Do you want me to do that?

Adoptee: No, that's okay. I feel better about it now. You can't blame me for being suspicious. At least, I'm honest about that. But, if everything is secret, then, I guess, I'm okay about it. (Fieldnotes, 3 July 1984: 22)

I believe that my professional stance made my presence more acceptable at these meetings. For example, I came to be known mainly as 'the girl doing research.' When I was introduced to adoptees in this manner they would ask questions about my research interests, and I would respond to their concerns immediately. The majority were positive towards my work because they believed my professional status would legitimate their own cause. To quote one long-term member, 'It's great that you're doing this. We need it. We can tell the story but no one will listen to it because we don't have the letters after our names. They will listen to you and what you have to say will carry more weight. Just ask me for any information that you want and I'll willingly help. I really believe in this and what you are doing' (Fieldnotes, 5 August 1984: 6). My role as a social researcher not only made my presence and 'odd' questions acceptable, but it offered members a 'safe haven' for their personal concerns (Lofland, 1971: 13). Often adoptees gave me information not discussed with other members. As one adoptee said, 'I tell you things because I can be comfortable with you. You are one of us but not one of us. I know that I can say things and you aren't shocked. You just accept them. I also know that nobody else will hear about it either. That makes it easier to talk to you' (Fieldnotes, 12 October 1984: 5). These types of contacts gave me a stronger understanding of the individual concerns and personal implications involved in the search for and contact with birth mother.

GAINING UNDERSTANDING THROUGH CONTINUOUS CONTACT

Parent Finders holds meetings once a month. Each meeting consists of a formal session where search techniques are outlined, advocacy issues are described, and newly reunited adoptees report on their experiences with contact with their birth mothers. Sometimes an adoptee may bring a birth relative or adoptive parent 'to show the group' or 'tell their part in the reunion story' (Fieldnotes, 7 September 1984: 12). Occasionally, a guest speaker from another group, an adoption agency, a counsellor, or a lawyer may give a lecture on adoption, search, or reunion issues. This formal session serves as an educational forum involving the organization's more global concerns. Information on adoption laws, legislative reforms, or political lobby activities is addressed as well as recent publications or media presentations on search and reunion. I believe that the group's exposure to these guest speakers prepared adoptees for my presence and made my research interest more acceptable to the Parent Finders membership.

When the formal session ends, the members divide themselves into smaller groups to assist each other with their individual search questions. Because many members socialize at this time, I talked with individual adoptees during this informal period. I also joined members after the meeting when they stopped at a coffee shop or restaurant to socialize. These informal discussions exposed me to a variety of Parent Finders members from whom I learned about the personal meaning of adoption, search, and desire for contact.

My continued attendance at Parent Finders meetings sensitized me to the motivations, expectations, and personal doubts experienced by adoptees who search for and establish contact with their birth mothers. The following fieldnote outlines a typical reunion scenario heard during the formal meeting session (3 July 1984). The sections in parentheses represent my own thoughts and observations.

(A woman of approximately 35 years of age is sitting on the stage with the executive members. She is introduced to us by the president as 'Mary, a newcomer who just joined and wants to tell us her story.')

Mary: I found my birth mother within a month of joining Parent Finders. (The audience gasps, probably because it usually takes months and often years to find someone and this is such a quick search.)

I have been looking much longer on my own without any help. (Most people smile and nod their head in agreement as if they had expected this. Many members try searches of their own before joining Parent Finders.)

I guess it really started in 1980 when I had my daughter. I was really angry. I had this reaction to my epidural and they kept saying, "How could she be so stupid?"

It was almost as if I wasn't there. As if I wasn't real or anything. They kept saying it. I got angry. They were right. I should have known.

After that, I sent away for my background information. I got two paragraphs. I was so thankful for that little bit. (People in the audience laugh.)

I read these two paragraphs for over two years. It was all that I felt that I was entitled to have. I found out that my birth father was Jewish. It made sense to me. I had done a minor in Jewish history at university. I guess this explained my attraction and my affinity to it because I was raised as an Irish Catholic. I never could understand why I was interested in that topic. Now, I knew. (Again, people nod and whisper to the person beside them.)

Then, my adoptive mother had a stroke about a year ago. She wanted to know what I wanted in the will because I hadn't asked for anything. I have four brothers who are her biological children. I always believed, in myself, that her children were the real heirs. (People in the audience whisper. Some smile and nod in agreement.)

I told her that I wanted my adoption papers. She got so upset that I thought she would have another stroke! (People in the audience laugh, shake their heads sympathetically.)

It took me another nine months to get them from her.

By this time, I was very angry! I felt that I had a right to know. I couldn't understand why my mother didn't want to help me.

We finally talked it all out. It turns out that her biggest fear was conversion! She knew about the Jewish part. (She laughs.) (The audience laughs with her.)

It was all so crazy really. (She shakes her head and shrugs her shoulders. So do many people in the audience.)

After a period of approximately three months, I realized that I was nodding, smiling, laughing, shrugging, and sighing at the same time and place as the Parent Finders audience. Like any other newcomer, I had slowly 'discovered the meanings' that composed the social world of the participants in my research (Lofland, 1971: 13).

From talking to other adoptees and listening to similar accounts, I began to understand that Mary's anger emerged from her sense of powerlessness over the closed awareness context that had placed her in a life-threatening position when she gave birth. By making Mary feel personally responsible for a situation over which she had no control, hospital personnel turned her anger towards herself ('I should have known'). That anger supported her desire for contact and prompted her to search ('they were right, I should have known').

Mary's initial request for genealogical and genetic background information produced two paragraphs. I learned at my first meeting that most adoptees receive less than this when they apply for non-identifying background information from the adoption agency. However, like Mary, they are 'thankful for that little bit' because they feel that it is all they are 'entitled to have'. Also, like Mary, these adoptees treasure each tiny piece of background material. Because most adoptees possess little or no genealogical information, each piece of information becomes a revelation that produces a stronger understanding about themselves. Thus, for example, Mary's pleasure over her Jewish heritage gave her a logical explanation for what had been viewed previously as 'illogical' behaviour (that is, why would a staunch Roman Catholic woman be attracted to Judaism?).

Like many other adoptees at these meetings, Mary expressed uncertainty about her status as a rightful heir to her adoptive parents' estate. She believed that her 'biological' brothers had a stronger claim. She interpreted her adoptive mother's reaction to her request for her adoption papers also as an unsympathetic response to her adopted status. However, once she and her mother discussed her reasons for searching, this initial anger disappeared and both women developed a stronger understanding of the other's position in the adoption triangle.

My research subjects' concerns became real to me because I observed *real* adoptees engaged in the process of the search and early contact with their birth mothers. I saw their expressions of frustration, pain, and joy when they tried to obtain access to bits and pieces of their genealogical background and knowledge of their birth mother's identity. I watched them laugh, cry, grow quiet and withdrawn, stamp their feet, or shout in glee as they encountered either unexpected barriers to access or discovered new background material. In this way, my period of participant observation at Parent Finders meetings gave me the understanding needed to conduct the next stage in my research project. That stage involved open-ended interviews with sixty adoptees who had been reunited for more than a year.

THE SEMI-STRUCTURED INTERVIEW APPROACH

Although my participant observation sessions at Parent Finders meetings provided considerable information on the search process, I soon discovered that few adoptees returned to the group once they had achieved contact with their birth mother. I had wanted originally to study the long-term effects of the outcome of reunion. When I found no existing support group of reunited adoptees to observe, I decided to conduct individual interviews. With this goal in mind I constructed a semi-structured interview questionnaire containing a combination of open and closed questions on search and reunion. Those questions focused on issues that emerged through my ob- servation sessions at Parent Finders and material found in the search and reunion research literature.

Semi-structured questionnaire interviews suffer from bias because research participants frequently distort reality or try to please the interviewer with the 'expected' response (Becker and Geer, 1957: 32). I believe, however, that my participant observation sessions helped me better judge my interviewees' answers. By comparing my interview data with my observations on adoptees in various stages of the search and early reunion process at Parent Finders meetings, I could evaluate the reliability of my interviewees' retrospective accounts more accurately. Also, my discussions with more established Parent Finders members who had observed many search and reunion experiences sensitized me to the subtleties of response that might have passed unnoticed in the interview session (Becker and Geer, 1957: 32).

A semi-structured interview schedule offers a flexible procedure at the same time as it presents a more organized and regular question format. The interviewer has the opportunity to probe, explore emerging issues, and extend the discussion into other relevant areas. Thus, for example, I saw many Parent Finders members express anger because adoptive parents' sig- natures were required before adoptees could register with the Ontario Re- union Registry. Although the interview questionnaire omits this topic, I probed it when it arose during interviews. Such probes occurred immediately before asking the next formatted question. The following interview section exemplifies this approach:

Researcher: Why was there a difference between the time that you decided to search and the time you began to search?

Adoptee: I was trying to get up enough nerve to ask my adoptive mother's permission.

Researcher: Why?

Adoptee: I don't know. She was always open about my adoption. I think that it was more from society. From other people. They view you as ungrateful if you want to know about your birth parents. I was afraid that she might think that way too. But, when I asked her to sign the papers for the Registry, she did. I wasted all of those years getting up the nerve to ask her. (She raises her voice, starts to shake.)

Researcher: You seem angry about that?

Adoptee: I was really angry. Here was my mother. She was ninety and living in an old-age home. I had power of attorney for her. I still had to go and ask her permission to register. Because, I wanted my search to be legal. Here I am. I am an adult and a grandmother. I had charge of her property and her bank account and all of her medical decisions. I am a professional woman. But, I had to ask my ninety year old mother's permission like a child. I was really angry. I still am when I think about it. It's not fair, really. In the eyes of the law, I will always be an adopted child. There is nothing I can do about it either. (Female adoptee, age 55)

In this way, each interviewed adoptee became an active participant in the interview process exploring issues of concern to them and raising subjects that I might have overlooked. In addition, at the end of each interview session, I asked these adoptees if there was anything that they wanted to discuss that had not been raised by the interview schedule or that they thought was an important part of search and reunion. This procedure allowed these adoptees greater control over their interview situation. For example, one adoptee replied, 'One thing specific that you didn't talk about was the birth father. I think he's just as important too because he is the other half. I think that if you want to discuss reunion that you should look at him too' (Male adoptee, age 34). As a result of that interview, I began to explore the topic of the birth father and the adoptee's interest in contact with him.

GAINING ACCESS TO AN INTERVIEW SAMPLE

Like other researchers interested in the outcome of reunion (Depp, 1982; Simpson et al., 1981; Sorosky et al., 1974; 1978; Stoneman et al., 1980; Thompson et al., 1978), I encountered great difficulty finding a sample of reunited adoptees to study. I had hoped to gain access to these adoptees through my observation sessions at Parent Finders meetings, but I soon realized that most reunited adoptees do not return to the group. Because meetings focus mainly on search techniques and early reunion contact, the recently reunited adoptees at Parent Finders offered me little information on the long-term outcome of contact with birth mothers. Oldtimer members presented a possible bias through their political activism in the group. I had to look elsewhere, therefore, for my interview sample.

When I mentioned my sampling difficulties to some Parent Finders members, they suggested that, because the Ontario Parent Finders organization had released their membership list to Sachdev for a survey study the previous year, their group might allow me access to their reunion list. I made a formal presentation to that group's executive board of directors outlining my research objectives. The Board released their reunion list to me as a sampling frame with my promise to maintain membership confidentiality. I believe that the board's contacts with me at Parent Finders meetings influenced their decision. They had learned to trust my professional ethics and my ability to maintain their members' integrity.

Each and every field study raises concern over ethical issues and the manipulation of research subjects to achieve research goals (Kirby and McKenna, 1989: 111–86; Neuman, 1994: 363–64). Every research study also entails risks for research participants who misinterpret the researcher's objectives (Barnes, 1963; Roth, 1960; Shaffir et al., 1980). Qualitative researchers are especially vulnerable to these risks because they engage in personal interaction with their research subjects. The research study becomes exploitative, however, only when the informant gains nothing or actually suffers harm from the research (Spradley, 1980: 24). Because both I and the Parent Finders executive had taken every possible precaution to ensure the confidentiality of the adoptees in this sampling frame, I believe that my method of contact did not place these adoptees at risk. Their positive attitude towards my research project supports my belief that they benefited also from their participation in the interviews.

DRAWING A SAMPLE AND RESPONSES OF INTERVIEWEES

This Parent Finders group reported 313 reunions for the period between June 1976 and January 1985, an average of thirty-nine reunions per year. Of those reunions, 223 (71 per cent) involved adoptees. The remainder included birth parents, adoptive parents or foster children as the primary searcher. Twenty-six (12 per cent) of those adoptee searches involved adoptees who lived outside of Ontario (e.g., New York, Manitoba, and Australia), and this distance factor eliminated those 26 from the list of possible interviewees. The remaining sampling frame consisted of 197 reunited adoptees.

On 25 March 1985 I randomly selected twenty-five names and mailed letters requesting an interview. The initial response to the letters was very encouraging. Within two weeks, six of the twenty-five adoptees called me to arrange an interview session. These callers expressed excitement over 'telling my story so others might understand' (Fieldnotes, 31 March 1985; 3 April 1985; 6 April 1985). Their enthusiasm exemplified the positive attitude presented by the majority of the interviewees involved in this study. To quote one of them, 'I think that it's just great that you are doing this. Because more people like me want to know. If you're going to do it then it's nice to know if your reunion is going the right way or not. Other people should know about it too so maybe they won't think it's so strange either' (female adoptee, age 23). Like many projects involving mailed-out material, the response rate was problematic (Neuman, 1994: 239). Nine of the first twenty-five letters were returned with 'no forwarding address' stamped on the envelope. In fear that confidentiality might be broken if I tried to find new addresses for these adoptees, I discarded their names. Over a six-month period, I drew ninety-seven names and sent letters requesting an interview. A total of thirty-one letters were returned with 'no forwarding address.' This number represented one-third of the drawn sample.

Of the remaining sixty-six adoptees who were contacted, six (9 per cent) declined an interview. Two adoptees said that they had 'little information to offer because my birth mother rejected me' (Fieldnotes, 6 August 1985: 1; 12 August 1985). One adoptee refused because her adoptive mother 'disapproved' and she 'wanted to respect [her] mother's feelings' (Fieldnotes, 15 July 1985: 1). Another adoptee cancelled her interview appointment because 'the idea of being interviewed raised a lot of painful memories that I'd just like to forget' (Fieldnotes, 18 May 1985: 1). One adoptee arranged an interview appointment but never arrived. During my follow-up call, a man answered the telephone and said, 'She doesn't want to be bothered with this stuff' (Fieldnotes, 17 June 1985: 1). I left the matter there. The remaining adoptee had died since her reunion (Fieldnotes, 22 May 1985: 1).

These refusals indicate a possible research bias whereby adoptees with a negative reunion outcome declined interviews. However, several of the interviewed adoptees reported painful reunion memories while eight had been rejected immediately by their birth mother. Others overcame possible family conflict by making special arrangements for their interview. For example, two of the adoptees met with me in a restaurant because their children did not know about their reunion. Another adoptee arranged his interview at my home because, 'Even though my parents know about it, it is a touchy subject and I don't want to remind them of it by having you come to their home' (Fieldnotes, 12 April 1985: 2). Except for these special requests, these adoptees could not be distinguished from the other interviewed adoptees. Their proposed solutions for overcoming their 'problematic' interview situations indicate a strong desire to engage in the research project.

GATEKEEPERS, BARGAIN MAINTENANCE, AND PARTICIPATION IN INTERVIEWS

Haas and Shaffir (1980: 245) describe the bargain stage of a research project 'as a series of negotiations throughout the research endeavour wherein the

researcher continually attempts to secure others' cooperation.' Most researchers bargain with gatekeepers who either control access to research
subjects or guarantee the research project's credibility (Douglas, 1976;
169–98; Neuman, 1994: 338–9). That research bargain consists of, 'an ex-
change relationship between the researcher and those studied. In return
for providing the researcher with information, respondents are guaranteed
confidentiality and anonymity, which encourage honest answers to questions'
(Shaffir et al., 1980: 26). Those adoptees who met me in restaurants exemplify the types of bargain agreements established between researchers
and research participants. The Parent Finders executive board represents
the gatekeepers who bargained with me over access to their reunion list.
During that bargaining process, the board removed the adoptive parents'
and birth parents' names from their reunion list because 'only the adoptees
were members of their organization and had placed themselves at risk for
further contact' (Fieldnotes, 8 February 1985). This bargain presented me
with a new dilemma. To gain access to these other research subjects, I had
to ask the adoptees' permission. The majority refused to release their adoptive parents' or their birth parents' names to me. Because I failed to negotiate
a successful bargain with these new gatekeepers, I had to abandon my original
research goal to examine the effects of contact for all three members of
the adoption triangle. Most of these adoptees denied me access to their
birth mothers because 'an interview would be too painful and humiliating
for her,' 'she hasn't told anyone about my existence and her privacy must
be protected,' or 'I promised I would never contact her again' (see Table
2.1). As a result, I received only eight names of birth mothers as potential
interviewees.

A similar pattern emerged when I asked for the names and addresses
of adoptive parents (see Table 2.2). A large number of these adoptees kept
their reunion secret from their adoptive parents because 'I didn't want to
hurt my parents' or 'I knew they couldn't handle the idea.' For similar reasons, others had postponed their search until after the deaths of their adoptive parents. The remainder claimed that the subject was 'too personal and
private for them to discuss with a stranger.' I received only eight names
of adoptive parents as possible interviewees.

This small sample of adoptive parents and reunited birth parents obtained
for this study made a comparative analysis of the effects of the outcome
of contact on all three members of the adoption triangle impossible. Their
protective action towards the release of the names of their adoptive parents
and birth parents is noteworthy, however. Contact with the birth mother
is not an isolated event. It involves all family members. Sachdev (1992: 65)

TABLE 2.1
Adoptees' response to researcher's request to interview birth mother
(rounded to nearest per cent) ($N = 60$)

Type of response	N	%
Permission given	8	13
Adoptee rejected	8	13
Birth mother found deceased	5	8
Birth mother deceased	2	3
Birth mother rejected	7	12
Limited contact or disengagement	7	12
Interview traumatic	12	20
Birth mother lives outside of province	2	3
Reunion too private	9	15
Total	60	99

and Pacheco and Eme (1993:61) note, for example, adoptees' preference
for relationships with birth siblings over relationships with birth mothers.
In addition, Stoneman et al. (1980: 14) and Sachdev (1992: 63) mention
the difficulty produced for the birth mother's husband when a birth child
from a prior relationship appears. These findings reveal a relationship between adoption, adoptive and birth family dynamics, and contact with the
birth mother that needs to be addressed more strongly in the research
literature.

CONSIDERATION OF THE SAMPLE

There are no formal statistics on the total number of adoptees in Canada
(Griffith, 1991; Hepworth, 1980) or the number of adoptees who seek contact with their birth mothers (Garber, 1985: 4; Gonyo and Watson,
1988: 16). The Ontario Parent Finders organization reported a membership
of 10,000 in 1984 (Fieldnotes, 5 June 1984). Twelve per cent (1,196) of
those members belonged to the Parent Finders group that offered its reunion
list for this study. Of those 1,196 members, only 780 (65 per cent) were
adoptees. Of those 780 adoptees, 223 (28.5 per cent) had achieved contact
with birth mothers. For reasons outlined previously, 197 of those reunited
adoptees formed the sampling frame used in this study.

To my knowledge, no other intensive examination on this number of
randomly selected reunited adoptees exists. The search and reunion literature
contains small, self-selected samples of volunteers obtained through media
appeals, social service agency clients, or members of activist search groups

TABLE 2.2
Adoptees' response to researcher's request to interview adoptive parent
(rounded to nearest per cent) ($N = 60$)

Type of response	N	%
Permission given	8	13
Not told of search	15	25
Died before search	10	17
Do not discuss search	8	13
Topic is private	9	15
Uncomfortable asking	5	8
Severed contact	3	5
Live outside province	2	3
Total	60	99

(Sachdev, 1989: 18). Sachdev (1992) offers the largest randomly selected
sample in his study of 124 Ontario Parent Finders members. However, his
use of a closed survey questionnaire hinders the exploration of topics not
identified by his interview schedule and 'forces respondents to give simplistic
responses to complex issues' (Neuman, 1994: 233). In contrast, the semi-
structured interview approach used in this study permits more 'creativity,
self-expression and richness of detail' (Neuman, 1994: 233) in the responses
of the interviewees.

Pacheco and Eme (1993) also examined a large randomly selected sample
of reunited adoptees (seventy-four) who were members of a search support
group in the United States. Like Sachdev, their use of a survey interview
questionnaire limits the qualitative analysis of their reunion findings. Yet,
these two studies offer a comparative baseline for evaluating the representativeness of the sample found in this study (Table 2.4–2.6). Also, because
this study sample was drawn from the same research population as Sachdev's
sample, each supports the reliability and validity of the other. The strong
association between this study sample and smaller volunteer samples taken
from social service agencies and reunion registries substantiates these findings further.

Pacheco and Eme (1993: 56) note the inherent bias existing in studies
containing members of support groups with strong advocacy positions who
'may feel more inclined to present a more positivist reaction toward the
reunion out of regard for the leaders or other members of the group.' This
was the major reason that I decided not to focus my study on oldtimer
Parent Finders members. The majority (52 or 86.6 per cent) of the reunited

TABLE 2.3
Years between adoptees' contact with birth mother and research interview
(rounded to nearest per cent) (*N* = 60)

Years	Males		Females		Total	
	N	%	N	%	N	%
<2	4	25	12	27	16	27
2 to 3	1	6	5	11	6	10
3 to 4	4	25	5	11	9	15
4 to 5	2	13	9	20	11	18
>5	5	31	13	30	18	30
Total	16	100	44	99	60	100

adoptees in this study sample discontinued contact with Parent Finders after they found their birth mothers. Their disengagement from that activist search organization offsets the bias that may emerge from their desire to support Parent Finders goals. That almost half of the sample (46.6 per cent) had experienced their reunion four years before their interview reduced the impact of the self-help search organization even further (see Table 2.3). I believe the reunion accounts presented in this study represent the adoptees' own perception of the search and the outcome of the reunion.

REPRESENTATIVENESS OF THE SAMPLE

Table 2.4 shows an age range of between twenty and fifty-nine years for this study sample; the median age is thirty-four. Although there are larger numbers of adoptees over the age of fifty and under the age of twenty-five than Sachdev or Pacheco and Eme report, this sample's ages fall within the range of the other two research studies. Also, despite the larger numbers of younger and older adoptees in this sample, analysis of the data reveals no association between age, motivation for the search, or reunion contact. It merely reaffirms the general research observation that interest in reunion may manifest itself at any period of an adoptee's life (Geidman and Brown, 1989: 19; Gonyo and Watson, 1988: 19; Schecter, 1964: 45; Simpson et al., 1981: 429).

Like the other two research samples, this study contains a large population (65 per cent) of married adoptees. This high degree of marital permanence contradicts the view of search and reunion as a symptom of the adoptee's social instability or disturbed state of mind (Clothier, 1943: 222; Sants,

TABLE 2.4
Comparison of sample characteristics with the sample characteristics
found by Sachdev (1992) and Pacheco and Eme (1993) (per cent)

Characteristics	Study sample ($N = 60$)	Sachdev ($N = 124$)	Pacheco & Eme ($N = 72$)
Gender			
Female	74.0	87.9	82.0
Male	26.0	12.1	18.0
Interview age			
<25	18.3	13.7	9.0
25 to 34	26.6	42.7	39.0
35 to 39	16.6	19.3	15.0
40 to 49	25.0	18.5	29.0
50+	13.3	6.7	8.0
Marital status			
Married	65.0	64.5	69.0
Separated, divorced or widowed	15.0	16.1	6.0
Never married	20.0	19.4	25.0

1965: 133; Toussieng, 1971: 323). Also, the sample's low rate of 'separated, divorced or widowed' adoptees (15 per cent) reflects the constancy in life experience and social stability that seems common among searchers (Anderson, 1989).

A similar sense of this sample's stability emerges in the education and employment patterns (see Table 2.5). Fifty-five per cent of these adoptees had received some post-secondary education or training and 31.7 per cent worked in professional, semi-professional or managerial occupations. The sizeable number of 'housewives' (26.7 per cent) reflects the predominance of female adoptees in the sample (74 per cent). The large percentage of 'clerical/sales' positions (23.3 per cent) may mirror the disproportionate number of women who occupy those types of positions in the paid labour force (Duffy and Pupo, 1992). These employment and educational patterns vary significantly from Sachdev's findings. Sachdev does not include a housewife category while 54.2 per cent of his sample were employed in 'clerical, sales and technical' occupations. Some of this variation may be the result of differences in coding techniques. Some of it may be determined by older members of this sample. Before the late 1960s and early 1970s, women became housewives upon marriage and were expected to remain in that role (Nett, 1993: 256–9). Upon retiring from the paid labour force, women may reclaim the label of 'housewife' as their major occupational role, while

TABLE 2.5
Comparison of sample characteristics with characteristics found by Sachdev (1992)
(per cent)

Characteristics	Sample (N = 60)	Sachdev (N = 124)
Employment		
Professional/semiprofessional	20.0	16.9
Clerical, sales, technical	23.3	54.2
Skilled, semiskilled, manual	5.0	20.6
Unskilled	3.3	8.4
Housewife	26.7	–
Student	10.0	–
Managerial	11.7	–
Household income		
<$12,000	8.3	10.3
$12,000 to $19,000	10.0	24.3
$20,000 to $34,999	65.0	33.6
$35,000 to $49,999	13.3	20.6
≥$50,000	3.0	11.2

men may be more likely to view themselves as 'retired' (Nett, 1993: 318–20). Since none of the adoptees in Sachdev's sample claimed to be 'retired,' and he does not use 'retired' in his classification scheme, more of his female adoptees may be shown as employed in 'clerical, sales and technical occupations' because their age range supports employment in the paid labour force.

This 'housewife' factor helps to explain some of the difference in the income levels reported by the two samples. The large percentage of adoptees (65 per cent) in this study sample who claimed a household income of between $20,000.00 and $34,999.00 may reflect single-income families. The sizable percentage of 'students' (10 per cent) in the study sample may have had an additional effect. Because the Parent Finders group providing the sampling frame exists close to a university, many of these students may be supporting themselves on student loans and part-time wages. This would lower the income categories demonstrated by those interviewees.

Although the data are not available in Pacheco and Eme's study, Sachdev (1992: 53) reports an Anglo-Saxon sample. The majority (90 per cent) of the sample in my study is also Anglo-Saxon. This finding is expected because these reunited adoptees belong to a branch group of the same self-help search organization. Moreover, the population of Ontario is predominantly

TABLE 2.6
Comparison of study sample's adoptive parent status with adoptive parent status
reported by Sachdev's sample at the time of interview (per cent)

Parental status	Study sample ($N = 60$)	Sachdev ($N = 124$)
Both parents alive and living together	43.4	48.6
Father deceased	25.0	15.9
Mother deceased	8.3	11.2
Both deceased	16.7	16.8
Separated or divorced	6.7	6.5

Anglo-Saxon. Thus, it is highly likely that this study sample matches the ethnic base of the adopted population of the province.

Like Sachdev's adoptees, this study sample reported stable adoptive family backgrounds (see Table 2.6). Over three-fourths had one or both adoptive parents living at the time they searched, and only 6.7 per cent experienced the conflict of parental divorce. Although three (5 per cent) had severed contact with their adoptive parents, these adoptees did not view their reunion as symptomatic of the adoption breakdown hypothesized by some researchers (Kadushin and Seidl, 1971; Lemon, 1959; McWhinnie, 1967; Triseliotis, 1973). To quote one of them, 'The thing about my adoptive parents is their drinking. It would have been there rather [sic] I had been adopted or not. It would have caused problems between us. It has nothing to do with my adoption or my search. I did it for other reasons' (female adoptee, age 29).

This lack of association between experience in adoptive families and desire for contact was supported by the sample's observations on their siblings. Forty (67 per cent) of these adoptees had siblings. Over one-half (twenty-one or 53 per cent) noted adoptive siblings who did not want to search (see Table 2.7). Although not part of the interview schedule, the topic of siblings was raised by these adoptees at different times in their interview session in response to a variety of questions about search and contact. Thus, for example, in describing her reunion outcome, one woman remarked that, 'I find it strange. My brother has talked about my search with me even though he doesn't want to search or meet his mother. He has no interest in it at all. I find that interesting because we have the same upbringing and similar lives. You would think that we would both want to do it' (female adoptee, age 36).

These sibling data support the reports of other researchers (Gonyo and Watson, 1988; Haimes and Timms, 1985; Pacheco and Eme, 1993; Sachdev,

TABLE 2.7
Adoptee siblings' desire for reunion (rounded to nearest per cent) ($N = 64$)

	Adoptees (N)	Male siblings	Female siblings	Total siblings
Biological siblings belonging to adoptive parents	17	20	16	36
	(43%)	(53%)	(62%)	(56%)
Siblings who searched	2	0	2	2
	(5%)	(0%)	(8%)	(3%)
Siblings who do not desire a search	21	18	8	26
	(53%)	(47%)	(31%)	(41%)
Total	40	38	26	64
	(101%)	(100%)	(101%)	(100%)

1992; Simpson et al., 1981; Sobol and Cardiff, 1983; Sorosky et al., 1974; Thompson et al., 1978) who note little relationship between search and negative outcome of adoption. If searching behaviour were symptomatic of adoption breakdown, then, it is likely that adopted siblings might use search also as a response to their dissatisfaction with the outcome of their adoption. These findings support the view that desire for contact is related more to perception of one's adoptive status than to structure of the adoptive family.

SIGNIFICANCE OF FEMALE SEARCHERS

The concept of gender emphasizes this relationship between perception of adoption and desire for contact more strongly than any of the other factors considered for this sample. Like the adoptees found in other search and contact studies, this sample reveals no significant pattern when measured on such traditional sociological categories as age cohort, religion, education, occupation, or income (Pacheco and Eme, 1993: 56). Gender is the only noticeable characteristic. There are approximately three times as many female adoptees (74 per cent) as male adoptees (26 per cent) in the study sample. This ratio mirrors the findings reported by other search and contact researchers (Depp, 1982; Gonyo and Watson, 1988; Haimes and Timms, 1985; Pacheco and Eme, 1993; Sachdev, 1992; Simpson et al., 1981; Sobol and Cardiff, 1983; Sorosky et al., 1974; Stoneman et al., 1980; Thompson et al., 1978). It appears that female adoptees desire contact with their birth mothers more than male adoptees.

Sobol and Cardiff (1983: 482) have hypothesized a methodological bias in search and contact studies whereby women are more prone to volunteer than men when requests are made for research subjects. However, the close similarity between the numbers of female (519 or 77 per cent) and male (152 or 23 per cent) searchers on the Parent Finders group membership list and the numbers of female (175 or 78 per cent) and male adoptees (48 or 22 per cent) on its contact list indicate a gender self-selection bias *before* the decision to search is made. Once males decide to search, they are just as likely as female searchers to achieve contact with their birth mothers.

Sorosky et al. (1974) suggest that this self-selection bias stems from women's personal connection to pregnancy and childbirth. Because women bear and rear children, they are more conscious of the 'continuity of life through the generations' (Sorosky et al., 1974: 20) that adoption eliminates. This hypothesis has been linked to childbirth as a specific life-change event activating search behaviour (Pacheco and Eme, 1993: 56; Sobol and Cardiff, 1983: 480; Thompson et al., 1978: 21). As well, many women experience medical interventions during pregnancy and delivery that may intensify their desire for more detailed medical information. Female adoptees may be more aware, therefore, of the serious, and possibly life-threatening, implications that their missing genetic information holds for both themselves and their children. This increased awareness may intensify the female adoptees' desire for contact. Mary, the adoptee who presented her story to the Parent Finders membership, exemplifies this situation very well.

Male adoptees may be less concerned with contact with their birth mother, however, because it involves a cross-gender relationship that holds little interest. If, as Sachdev (1992: 58) suggests, male adoptees express more concern about their birth fathers, then the saliency of the birth mother's role in the adoption process may dissuade them from searching. I heard this concern expressed, for example, at Parent Finders when a young male adoptee attending his first meeting told me, 'Everyone seems to be concentrating on the birth mother. No one seems to ask about the birth father or want to make any connections with him. I just wanted to find out who he is. I didn't think I would have to find her too' (Fieldnotes, 7 June 1984, 17). When told that, practically, he would have to make an initial contact with his birth mother, because 'only she really knows the birth father's identity,' the man left and never appeared at any further meetings I attended.

Also, the saliency of the birth mother's position in the adoption process may affect the disproportionate number of female searchers in a more subtle way. It is important to note that the 'culture of women' centres around the role of 'mother' (Rich, 1986: xxviii). Female adoptees who become 'mothers' may gain more empathy, therefore, for the social position of a woman who bears a child out of wedlock. The following two quotes describe this attitudinal difference between genders. One male adoptee explained, for example, that, 'In order to search, I had to get over the feelings that she gave me up. I believe that if you have a kid you should be able to look after it. I would never let anyone take a kid from me. I wouldn't have one unless I could look after it. But, my wife made me realize that in those days women had no support. They couldn't get jobs. You were looked down upon if you had an illegitimate child. When I got my background information, I realized that my wife was right. She had to do what she did. When I met her, all those bad feelings went away because I knew that she did care about me' (male adoptee, age 24). In contrast, a female adoptee noted, 'After my daughter was born and loving her the way that I loved her, I couldn't believe that someone would have done that and not wondered or had feelings like "My God, what have I done? I hope it turned out for the best". In the back of my mind, I felt that there was someone out there that wondered if she had done the right thing and I wanted to tell her that she had' (female adoptee, age 32).

Yet, the role of 'mother' involves more than childbearing. Women serve as the primary caregivers who nurture and socialize the children (Levine and Estable, 1990). Women are responsible, also, for the maintenance of family health, family rituals and family ties (Rich, 1986). This role gives women a stronger sense of the importance of genetic heritage and a more powerful need for a genealogical background of their own. Within the social context of home and family, women are more likely also to encounter social interactions in which their lack of background information becomes problematic for a satisfactory presentation of self. In this way, the social position occupied by women in a world divided by gender may increase the female adoptee's need for contact with her birth mother relative to her male counterpart, who exists mainly within a social world based on occupational structure and individual achievement (Fox, 1993; Nett, 1993).

The data in this book come from two sources. The first source consists of an extensive fifteen-month period of participant observation at meetings held by two Ontario Parent Finders groups. The sympathetic understanding developed through those observation sessions helped in the construction of the open-ended interview schedule used in this study. This second source provides the material analysed in the following chapters.

Gaining access to a research sample of reunited adoptees presented some difficulty. However, the trust and rapport developed between me and members of the Parent Finders executive board led to the release of a contact list that served as the sampling frame. Names were randomly selected from that contact list and introductory letters mailed to prospective interviewees. Those letters elicited an interview sample of sixty adult adoptees who had been reunited for at least one year.

My participant observation sessions at Parent Finders meetings strengthen the reliability and validity of the responses in this study sample. The similarity between social characteristics in this sample and those found in other search and contact studies supports it as well. Like those in other research samples, these adoptees revealed no significant relationship between their socioeconomic characteristics, their search, or the outcome of their contact. The only noticeable sociological categories were the large number of females in the sample and adoption.

It is important to note that the predominance of female adoptees in this sample indicates a self-selection bias that takes place *before* the decision to search is made. The male adoptees in this study experienced similar search paths, used the same types of search tactics, and demonstrated comparable reactions to their search and contact findings as did their female counterparts. For this reason, gender fades in the data analysis presented in the following chapters. When gender distinctions do occur, they emphasize the separate social realities experienced by men and women who exist in a society that discriminates on the basis of gender.

This book repeats much of the same material explored in other studies of search and contact. It examines adoptees' motivations to search, their decision to search, their initial contact with their birth mothers, and the possible development of a long-term adoptee–birth mother relationship. The issue of search for and contact with birth mothers is, however, a relatively new area of interest in the field of adoption research. Repetition of similar data validates prior research findings on this very important social issue.

The data also contain some of the limitations encountered in the research literature. The study explores personal, retrospective accounts of the search and reunion process. It does not contain a control group of non-searching, non-reunited adoptees. Its strength lies with the random selection of a large sample of adoptees who provide extensive accounts of their search and outcome of contact. Those accounts present an intimate view of search and contact with birth mothers that enlightens us all.

3

Desire for Contact with Birth Mothers and the Reflected Appraisals of Others

The sixty reunited adoptees in this study relate similar concerns about identity in their accounts of search and contact as those reported in the research literature. They extend that analysis, however, through their description of the social effects of secrecy in adoption. The closed awareness context surrounding the adoptees' genealogical and genetic backgrounds creates biographical discontinuities that bring into question their satisfactory presentation of self. The adoptees' attempt to remove these biographical discontinuities through contact with their birth mothers provides the major motivation for their search and a prime consideration in satisfaction with reunion.

SELF AND IDENTITY AS SOCIAL PRODUCTS

Central to the theoretical understanding of search and reunion is the view of self and identity as social products created and maintained through social interaction with others (Meltzer et al., 1975; Rosenberg, 1981). According to Mead (1934: 38), self is unique from all other social objects because 'it can become an object unto itself.' By 'taking the role of the other,' we, as individuals, enter our own experience of self indirectly through the standpoint of those others (Blumer, 1969: 60–77; Cooley, 1902: 183–4; Mead, 1934: 137–8). We see ourselves as separate objects because others identify, label, describe, and act towards us in special ways. The development of *self* requires, therefore, an awareness of the existence of others and the ability to continually observe, reflect upon, and take into account those other perspectives (Mead, 1934: 164).

The more people we meet, the more diversified and complex our view of self becomes. We maintain a stable image of self or *personal identity*, however, through the continuity of experiences encountered throughout our lives and the consistency of others' responses to us (Shibutani, 1961: 216, 239). Because we can never enter other people's minds, our personal identity takes the form of a 'looking glass self' (Cooley, 1902: 184) reflecting our imagination of how others perceive us. These 'reflected appraisals' produce feelings about self, such as shame or pride, which influence that view (Cooley, 1902: 239). In this way, our perception of others' reactions to us, and our feelings about those reactions, affect our personal identity (that is, our view of self) much more than others' actual behaviour towards us.

Possession of a personal identity lets us enter situations with parts of self already established. However, because others certify our view of self when they accept the signs and symbols that we present, our personal identity becomes 'situated' in the momentary process of social interaction (Stone, 1962: 93; Alexander et al., 1981: 269–89). Knowing the social situation and the identities of others before we interact helps us, therefore, to arrange our own behaviour more appropriately (Stryker, 1980: 54; Thomas, 1931). The stronger the presentation of self we achieve, the more likely the 're-flected appraisals' of others will affirm our personal identity.

To gain more accurate definitions of the situation, we create biographies of others that we draw upon for interactional reference. These biographies result mainly from others' self-disclosures and documentary evidence pre-sented to us. We use this biographical information to assess others' *social* identity, that is, the particular category of people to which they belong. Then we orient our presentation of self around that social identity. For this reason, the information contained in others' biographies and the con-nectedness of that information is very important to us.

People who do not offer us precise biographical information present us with 'biographical discontinuities' that, if discovered, undermine our trust in the identity that they present. Such people are 'reduced in our minds from a whole and usual person to a tainted, discounted one' (Goffman, 1963: 3). The 'special discrepancy' between their *virtual* social identity (that is, who they appear to be) and their *actual* social identity (that is, who they are really) becomes a focus of our attention that must be explained (Goffman, 1963: 3). Because their special discrepancies disrupt the process of interaction, we discredit their presentation of self and discriminate against them for contradicting our expectations of who we expect them to be. In this way, people with biographical discontinuities carry a 'social stigma' or discreditable flaw that disqualifies them from full social acceptance (Gof-fman, 1963: 1).

Each 'biographical discontinuity' has the potential to expose people to social stigma as someone different than expected (Goffman, 1963: 3). The precariousness of their potentially embarrassing position varies with the number of discontinuities in their biography, the centrality of that information for smooth social interaction, the number of others who know about the discontinuity, and the regularity with which this potentially discrediting information can be drawn into the process of social interaction. The more frequently a biographical discontinuity arises to dispute others' social assumptions, the stronger the social sanctions imposed.

This theoretical paradigm summarizes the social position occupied by people who experience secrecy in adoption. Non-disclosure surrounds adoptees' genealogical and genetic backgrounds within a closed awareness context that creates biographical discontinuities and exposes them to social discrimination by others. The adoptees who were interviewed for this study outlined this discrimination process in their accounts of adoption, search and reunion. They described how others' reactions to their biographical discontinuities affected their view of self and stimulated their desire for contact with their birth mothers. Those descriptions revealed a search motivation that considers more fully the link between the identity 'gaps' created by non-disclosure and the need to 'fill in' those gaps. These adoptees wanted to neutralize the social stigma of their adoption by gaining personal control over the release of private information about self.

PERCEPTION OF ADOPTION AS SOCIAL STIGMA

The sixty adoptees in this study expressed motivations for search similar to those found in the search and contact literature (see Table 3.1). Like other searchers, they wished for more complete genealogies; expressed curiosity over the events surrounding their conception, birth and relinquishment; wanted information that could be passed down to their children; and yearned for more detailed knowledge of their biological family background (Gonyo and Watson, 1988; Haimes and Timms, 1985; Pacheco and Eme, 1993; Sachdev, 1992; Simpson et al., 1981; Sobol and Cardiff, 1983; Sorosky et al., 1974; Triseliotis, 1973). However, their explanations of these motivations also revealed a strong image of adoption as social stigma. For example, one man stated, 'Those feelings of not belonging that I developed. I don't think that they were necessarily formed on my own. They were inflicted on me from the outside. That negative message and reaction that you got whenever the topic of adoption was brought up. I soon learned never to volunteer the information that I was adopted to anyone unless I was asked directly. I didn't want to be thought of as different from the rest' (male, age 35). Another woman declared, 'People always react to the news that you are adopted. Because there is a slight shame to being adopted. Not everybody else is adopted. Everybody else has their real parents. Why don't you? There must be something wrong. If other people are nice or not, they see you as different' (female, age 43).

To support their description of adoption as social stigma, these adoptees mentioned specific incidents of social discrimination by others who knew of their adoptive status. Of particular note were personal slights by extended adoptive family members who advised them to 'be grateful you were taken in by such loving parents,' referred to them as 'the adopted one,' or excluded them from family functions such as weddings or graduation parties that included biological relatives of their own age. Four adoptees had received no inheritance from adoptive grandparents because they were 'not blood relatives.' One adoptee observed that her adoptive uncle stopped his family tree at her adopted father's name 'because the blood line ended there.' These adoptees believed that this discrimination by extended family members reflected their stigmatized status within the larger community. One claimed that, 'You experience prejudice in subtle ways. I remember when my brother-in-law's son was getting married. They had to cut the list down. There was a cousin in the family who had two adopted children. They said that they would cut the children off the list because they weren't really family anyway. You sit there. You listen. You think, that's what they are probably saying about you when you aren't around. You're never really fully accepted by people. If family feels that way, you can count on others to be the same' (female, age 54).

Examples of this type arose spontaneously throughout the interview session as these adoptees discussed their desire for contact with their birth mothers. The most dramatic incidents were childhood events in which these adoptees first became aware of adoption as social stigma. For instance, one woman described a continuous process of childhood ridicule that deeply affected her view of self. She said, 'Being adopted was hard. As a young kid, the other kids called you a bastard. I would try to ignore it. But it was a fact of life. I was adopted. I couldn't change that. I had to deal with it. That was just part of my experience. They would try to put you down so you never tried to put yourself up. I never tried to be class president or spokesperson or that. I felt it wasn't my right. And, I never got picked for things. I always felt that my social standing was such that adopted children wouldn't get picked. That they weren't good enough. I guess that still holds today. I still have to push myself because I feel that people will think that I shouldn't try for things. That I don't deserve it because I'm adopted' (fe-

TABLE 3.1
Adoptees' reasons for desire to search for their birth mothers (rounded to nearest per cent)

Reason	First response						Second response						Third response						Total response					
	Males		Females		Total		Males		Females		Total		Males		Females		Total		Males		Females		Total	
	N	%	N	%	N	%	N	%	N	%	N	%	N	%	N	%	N	%	N	%	N	%	N	%
Genealogical curiosity	4	25	11	25	15	25	6	40	15	46	21	44	2	22	3	17	5	19	12	29	29	31	41	30
Medical history	1	6	6	14	7	12	2	13	8	24	10	21	1	11	5	28	6	22	4	10	19	20	23	17
Who do I look like?	6	38	12	27	18	30	2	13	1	3	3	6	1	11	4	22	5	19	6	15	17	18	23	17
More in-depth information about 'roots'	0	0	9	21	9	15	1	7	2	6	3	6	2	22	2	11	4	15	3	7	13	14	16	12
Out of place in adoptive family	2	13	2	5	4	7	0	0	0	0	0	0	1	11	0	0	1	4	3	7	2	2	5	4
Want to meet and talk with birth mother	3	19	4	9	7	12	4	27	7	21	11	23	2	22	4	22	6	22	13	32	15	16	28	21
Total	16	101	44	101	60	101	15	100	33	100	48	100	9	99	18	100	27	101	41	100	95	101	136	101

male, age 55). Yet, this message of being socially stigmatized through adoption did not always require repetition. A young man replied, 'I only remember one incident that sticks out in my mind. It was from a child about four or five years old. I think I was seven. He said, "You're adopted. You're not real. I was born. You weren't. You were adopted." I replied, "I was born too." He said, "Prove it." I couldn't. That's the only incident that I remember my adoption being brought up in a negative way and it was from a little kid who didn't know any better. But, it made me realize that I was different' (male, age 25). Also, such events were not isolated to other children. Thus, a young woman observed, 'I don't think that it really hit home until, in grade eight, my principal told me that I was probably getting into trouble at school because I was adopted. I'll never forgive him for that. I had problems because of my parents' drinking. He made me feel it was me. Because I was adopted' (female, age 28).

The adoptees in this study viewed these childhood events as the beginning stage in a lifelong process of social discrimination through adoption. Although they described some of their discriminatory encounters as minor annoyances, they were more emotional about others. Thus, they perceived requests for background information on application forms as small reminders of their missing genealogical and genetic backgrounds. However, they considered others' speculations about their birth mothers' morality or the strength of their adoptive parent–child bonds a personal insult. The following woman illustrated the various levels of this process of social discrimination when she described adoption as 'a recurrent theme in your life. You face it at different times and at different levels. In school, when they do a family tree, which family do you choose? In your teens, when you start talking about sex and you learn how babies are made. You are given this image that girls who have babies and are not married are bad. They are sluts. You get that idea about your birth mother. Then, you get married and have children of your own. Where did you come from? What is your background? But, it's not just that. It can come up anytime. When you're talking to the neighbours and they ask about your background and you say that you're adopted. You see the look on their face. They never thought that you were like that. Adopted. Different. Not like them' (female, age 19).

In this way, these adoptees perceived that others in their community viewed them differently for being adopted. Repeated encounters with others' negative reactions to their adoptive status reinforced that perception. Because those 'reflected appraisals' transmitted feelings of shame to self for being adopted, these adoptees viewed their adoptive status as a stigma trait that had to be managed. Effective management of that stigma trait was difficult, however, because of the biographical discontinuities produced by non-disclosure. They could never be certain about what types of background information might be requested or how their adoptive status might be drawn into the process of social interaction.

BIOGRAPHICAL DISCONTINUITIES, CLOSED AWARENESS CONTEXTS, AND UNSATISFACTORY PRESENTATIONS OF SELF

In their accounts of search and contact, these adoptees described specific times when their biographical discontinuities had discredited their presentation of self. They noted also that their inability to provide an adequate account of those biographical discontinuities increased others' concern over their 'real' (that is, actual) identity. For example, in her explanation of her desire for contact with her birth mother, one woman remarked, 'Not knowing things about yourself makes it so you don't belong. Like, my nationality. Everybody has a background. They're Italian, English, Jewish or whatever. I couldn't say what mine was. If anyone mentioned my nationality, they would start to guess. Because I didn't know. It became a real topic of conversation. A guessing game. Sometimes it would last and last. It wouldn't go away. I wished I knew just so it would stop' (female, age 36). Another woman replied, 'There were little details that were missing that other people know automatically. People grow up knowing their birth weight or the time when they were born. If the subject ever came up, I had to explain why I didn't know. Like horoscopes. I could never get a real one done because I don't know what time I was born. Do you know how often people talk about horoscopes? Stupid little things like that. I guess it shouldn't matter but it does' (female, age 35). At such times, to save their presentation of self, these adoptees announced their adoptive status to others. However, by drawing attention to their adoptive status, their biographical disconti-nuities exposed them as people who were 'different' from others' expec-tations of them (Goffman, 1963: 3). Thus, one young man said that, 'there are times when it comes up that you are adopted. You have people being surprised because they thought that you were normal. Like everyone else. You have to explain your situation. It became a routine. A part of me. Some-thing I had to cope with. Everyone has things that they have to cope with. This was mine' (male, age 28). In this way, others' curiosity over these biographical discontinuities reinforced the adoptees' perception of adoption as social stigma.

During such social situations, these adoptees found that the closed awareness context created by non-disclosure made them vulnerable to an intense process of public scrutiny. They could not satisfy others' requests for more complete information about self because they did not have any. Often, others refused the adoptees' explanation of adoption and transformed the interactional context into a suspicion awareness context. They would either speculate about the adoptees' actual identity or blame them for their lack of information. This new interactional context discredited these adoptees further. One particular interaction of this type occurred frequently with 'doctors and medical students who always ask about your family background. When you say that you are adopted, they ask "What difference does that make?" They don't understand. If they're not involved themselves, they don't realize that adoptees can't gain this information. They kept asking like I was hiding it or something. They wouldn't believe I didn't have anything. Nothing. No family history. They think it's my fault' (female, age 41). At other times, the adoptees' identity was discounted entirely. Thus, one woman remembered, 'When my son was born, my husband's mother said, "Oh, he has long fingers like Aunt A." I thought, "I have long fingers, too. Give me some credit." I was treated like I didn't have anything to offer because they weren't sure where it came from. Even what they could see, they wouldn't accept as real. Part of me wanted to find out for those reasons, too' (female, age 52).

This perception of not satisfying others' expectations produced shameful feelings about their adoptive status and their presentation of self. Many of these adoptees, therefore, avoided social situations that might produce these interactional contexts. Like the following woman, they refrained from attending, 'birthday parties and baby showers. Sometimes even weddings. Family things like that. People start talking about their children and their relatives. Everyone around you can relate their children and themselves to other members of their family. They say, "He acts like Uncle Joe." Things like that. I can't do that with myself or with my children. Our heritage was taken away from us for good reasons. But, when you take that away from a person, you are taking away a lot that you really don't know about. Events like that reminded me. I tried not to go (female, age 48). Such avoidance techniques were ineffective for these adoptees, however, because they could never predict 'when the subject might come up, just casually, in conversation.' This lack of control over the interactional situation created difficulty for an effective management of their stigma trait and a satisfactory presentation of self. These adoptees experienced little affirmation, therefore, from others for their personal identity as adoptees. In addition, the suspicion awareness contexts produced by others' curiosity over their 'real' identity raised personal concern about the authenticity of that adoptive identity. That concern was expressed through the question 'Who am I?'

INTERNALIZATION OF SOCIAL STIGMA, DOUBTS ABOUT PERSONAL IDENTITY, AND THE NEED FOR A BIOLOGICAL CONNECTION

Like others in their community, these adoptees questioned the legitimacy of their self-presentation when their biographical discontinuities intruded upon the process of social interaction. Because they lacked the facts needed to counterbalance the negative effects of those biographical discontinuities, they could not manage their self-presentations effectively. Repeated encounters with others' reactions to their adoptive status produced a personal sense of uncertainty about those unknown parts of self. Thus, like others, these adoptees questioned the possibility that they might be someone other than who they appeared to be. Any noticeable distinction between self and other adoptive family members supported those doubts. In this way, the question, 'Who am I?', became a topic of concern for these adoptees. One claimed, for example, that, before reunion, 'I would find myself doing things and thinking a certain way that I know darn well wasn't the line of thinking in my family. I would wonder why was I thinking that way? What was it about me that made me different in that way? I figured I wasn't quite the person that everyone thought me to be. It had to be my heredity. I wondered who I was really' (female, age 49).

The nature–nurture debate is well known. It holds particular meaning, however, for adoptees who lack precise information on their genealogical and genetic background (Sachdev, 1992; Sorosky et al., 1974). The adoptees in this study centred doubts about their identity around that debate. They experienced uncertainty over their adoptive identity because they could not substantiate which of their characteristics were based on 'nurture' and which on 'nature.' In this way, their missing biological ties became the 'objective basis' of their social stigma (Goffman, 1963: 5). These adoptees believed that, as the source of their 'natural' traits, the birth mother could verify their 'real' identity. Thus, when asked to explain his desire for contact, one man replied, 'I needed a connection. There was a vacuum there. I think that maybe what I was doing was trying to get some information to fill in that gap. That vacuum was that I was unrelated to people. I didn't have any ties or connections to anyone in this world other than myself. My adoptive parents. My wife and children. It's different somehow. I think that I was looking for an anchor. To make myself seem real somehow' (male, age

31). This man's need for a biological connection could not be filled by his adoptive parent ties, his marriage ties, or his own parent–child ties. Those ties been established under different circumstances and carried other social expectations. Like the other adoptees in this study, he had perceived that, without an original biological connection, 'as an adoptee, you're always on the outside. When you're growing up. Everybody says, "B's got X's eyes" or "He acts just like D." The adoptee is never a part of those things. There is always this cut-off point. Even, if it's not intentional. It's always there. You're not a part of the in-crowd. That's a lot of it. Wanting to feel a part of it. To be like everybody else. You want something that is biologically yours' (female, age 35).

This need for an original biological connection gained more prominence for these adoptees when they considered the source of their physical characteristics or temperament. Yet, their concern over the source of those attributes symbolized much more than genetic or genealogical curiosity. Whether intentional or not, social interactions involving inherited family traits exclude adoptees. Such interactions emphasize further their social stigma as people who are other than they appear to be. This situation was described effectively by a young man who had been matched so closely with his adoptive mother that others believed her to be his biological mother. In this way, this adoptee's strong physical resemblance to his adoptive mother became a focus of attention because she was *not* the biological source of those characteristics. He explained that, 'I searched because I wanted to know where my looks came from. In a way, that's crazy because my adoptive mother and I look so much alike. Everyone was always surprised when they found out I was adopted. In fact, at one time, I wondered if she was lying to me about it. But, I still wanted to know where I got my looks from. Funny, eh? I needed to know that someone out there looked like me' (male, age 21). This man reveals the identity confusion produced by secrecy in adoption. His observations demonstrate also the adoptees' sense of distrust in their adoptive identity. This adoptee had been told that his adoptive mother was not the source of his physical characteristics. Yet, because he lacked a full account of that source, he questioned whether she was lying to him about his adoption. He had to accept his mother's definition of the situation, however, because it was the only one available to him. For this adoptee, the question, 'Who do I look like?' reinforced the question, 'Who am I?'. His strong physical resemblance to his adoptive mother had transformed the closed awareness context produced by non-disclosure into a suspicion awareness context in which he as well as others questioned both his own and his mother's 'real' identity. This social situation strengthened his uncertainty about his adoptive identity and his feelings of powerlessness over his presentation of self.

Although not as emphatic as this man's example, all of the adoptees in this study had engaged in suspicion awareness contexts in which they speculated about either their own or others' true identity. For example, many had wondered if certain relatives or close family friends might be their biological parents. Others had avoided dating relationships 'in case the person was my brother and I didn't know it.' A large number had questioned 'if this person was acting nice to me because she knew who I really was.' These suspicion awareness contexts demonstrate the doubts about personal identity produced for adoptees who lack complete genealogical and genetic backgrounds. The adoptees in this study had internalized the uncertainty expressed by others over their 'real' identities and transformed it into doubts about their personal identities as adoptees. They saw contact with their birth mothers as a way to remove those doubts and gain a biological connection that would substantiate the source of their inherited traits.

Often, to counteract the effects of their social stigma, these adoptees had engaged in pretence awareness contexts in which they professed to be what others expected them to be (Goffman, 1963: 3). These types of social interactions involved mostly family functions or social situations requiring vague disclosures about one's family relationships. During such events, these adoptees took on the identity of a person who possessed biological family connections. Performance of that identity reminded them, however, of their more questionable birth identity. Thus, one woman remarked, 'You hear all your friends talk about their cousins or grandparents. You talk about your cousins also. But, you always know that they aren't your cousins. Not really. There was always that "really." I felt a bit like a fraud' (female, age 33). These types of experiences reminded these adoptees of their questionable status as 'people who are not who they appear to be' (Goffman, 1963: 3).

The adoptees in this study realized that the birth mother could place them within a biosocial context. They transformed their desire for an original biological connection, therefore, into a desire for contact with the birth mother. The birth mother was present during the events of their conception, birth, and relinquishment. She signed the legal papers releasing them for adoption. When they established contact with the birth mother, they would gain irrefutable proof of their biological connection to others and undisputed knowledge of their genealogical and genetic background. In this way, the birth mother became the symbolic representation of their missing genealogical background and contact with their birth mother became the ultimate goal of their search.

DESIRE FOR REUNION, POSTPONEMENT OF THE SEARCH, AND THE DECISION TO REUNITE

Despite their reported need for contact with the birth mother, almost half (29 or 48 per cent) of these adoptees had delayed their search for more than ten years after they expressed their first desire for reunion. (see Tables 3.2 and 3.3). In an attempt to discover the reasons for this postponement of the search, adoptees were asked the question, 'Why do you think that you waited until you were "XX" years of age to search when you began to think about searching earlier?' Table 3.3 shows their responses.

Seventeen (15 per cent) of these adoptees' responses about postponement consider the early inception of the desire for reunion. Because thirty-eight (64 per cent) of these adoptees reported their first thoughts of reunion during childhood, this reason for postponement seems appropriate. Also, most adoptees experience an inordinate interest in their genealogy as they struggle with the identity transition required during adolescence (Sants, 1965: 134; Toussieng, 1962: 65). Adoptees' genealogical curiosity may be noted, therefore, but not seriously acknowledged by others as a serious search request. Unless adolescent adoptees gain support from a sympathetic adult, their relatively powerless position as minors makes it almost impossible for them to initiate serious search action. Both of the reunited adoptees in this sample who achieved reunion contact before the age of twenty were assisted, for example, by their adoptive mothers.

A noticeable number (twenty-one or 19 per cent) of postponement responses involved the adoptees' lack of knowledge about search. The legal and normative sanctions held against reunion discouraged these adoptees from openly expressing their desire for contact with the birth mother. Until they encountered some positive endorsement of search through a television information program, reading material on the topic, or a sympathetic other, they did not view contact as a reality. Thus, one woman remarked, 'There was not a place for me to search. I hadn't the foggiest idea of how to go about it. I didn't think that I should for one thing. I thought that I was alone in these thoughts. That this was a bad thing to do. Disrespectful of my parents. Things like that. When I found out that there were many others out there who would like to search and some who had reunited, then, I didn't feel guilty about wanting to do it' (female, age 49).

Nineteen (17 per cent) of the responses about postponement fell under the category 'life kept getting in the way.' Many of these adoptees believed that the legal restrictions of non-disclosure would impede their search. Oth-

TABLE 3.2
Years between adoptees' thought and action regarding the search for the birth mother
(rounded to nearest per cent) (N = 60)

Years difference	Males		Females		Total	
	N	%	N	%	N	%
Zero*	5	31	9	21	14	23
1 to 9	6	38	11	25	17	28
10 to 19	3	19	9	21	12	20
20 to 29	2	13	15	34	17	28
Total	16	101	44	101	60	99

*Zero indicates a person who took immediate action when he or she became conscious of the
desire for contact with the birth mother (rounded to nearest per cent).

ers noted previous half-hearted and undirected search attempts that had
demonstrated the amount of time and energy required for completion of
the search. Search demands a commitment of self. Because their biographical
discontinuities did not obstruct their participation in most social activities
(Haimes and Timms, 1985: 51; Simpson et al., 1981: 432; Triseliotis,
1973: 172–3), these adoptees had placed greater priority on fulfilling more
immediate life goals such as marriage, child-rearing, and occupational advancement. A young woman summarized this postponement position when
she replied, 'I don't think that I was ready when I was eighteen. Then,
the next ten years, I was so busy with my life. My life was constantly changing. I got married. I had my son. I got a job. I really didn't have time
to look for her. And, I really didn't want to take the time because I knew
that it would probably involve a lot of time to search. That's mainly why
I postponed it. But, when I was turning thirty-two, I had all the time in
the world. I wasn't working. I thought that I would do it now because maybe
next year, I wouldn't have the time again' (female, age 34).

These reasons for postponement of search provide an understanding of
the serious decision-making process required before search can be initiated.
From an early age, these adoptees had internalized their stigmatized adoptive
status as a part of self. They were familiar with the sense of uncertainty
created by their missing genealogical and genetic background. Delaying the
search maintained the status quo. In contrast, search for and contact with
birth mothers presented considerable uncertainty. Fifty per cent of the reasons given for postponement of the search fell, therefore, under the category
of 'fear, concern, and apprehension.'

TABLE 3.3
Adoptees' reasons for postponement of the search (rounded to nearest per cent) (*N* = 113)

Reason given	First response		Second response		Third response		Total	
	N	%	N	%	N	%	N	%
Too young	12	20	2	5	3	19	17	15
Life got in the way	12	20	4	11	3	19	19	17
Fear	26	43	22	60	8	50	56	50
Don't know	10	17	9	24	2	13	21	19
Total	60	100	37	100	16	101	113	101

Table 3.4 describes the components of this fear. These adoptees reported delay in search because of their 'fear of hurting my adoptive parents,' 'fear of rejection,' 'fear of breaking society's norms,' 'fear of disrupting the birth mother's life,' and 'fear of the search results.' These fears were difficult to isolate or prioritize. A typical response to this question was, 'I was a bit scared about what I might find out. That I might not like it. But hoping that I would be happy with it. There is always that fear. Say, you find them and meet them and she's married and she's got children. How are you going to handle it? They also might reject her because of that. It's a very touchy thing. She might reject me. You never know what you are going to find. There are so many things to consider' (male, age 59).

The strongest deterrent to search was 'fear of hurting the adoptive parents' (fourteen or 25 per cent). These adoptees claimed strong adoptive parent–child bonds. They worried, therefore, about the impact of search and reunion on their adoptive parent–child relationship. This fear was so strong that, as noted in the previous chapter, ten (17 per cent) of these adoptees did not search until after their adoptive parents' deaths (see Table 2.2). Fifteen others (25 per cent of the sample) reunited without telling their adoptive parents of their contact with the birth mother. This secrecy in search reflected the closed awareness context created by these adoptive parents whenever the topic of their adoption was raised. Thus, one of the adoptees who kept her search activities secret from her adoptive parents, observed that 'I didn't want to hurt my mother or father. I know that they wouldn't have taken kindly to it. So, I didn't do anything until after they had died. My mother was very insecure about my adoption. She never liked to talk about it. I know that if I had ever approached her about searching that she would have thought that I didn't have any feelings for her any more. That's not the case. I just wanted to know something about the person

TABLE 3.4
Adoptees' postponement of search and fear of outcome of search (rounded to nearest per cent)
($N = 56$)

Fear	First response		Second response		Third response		Total	
	N	%	N	%	N	%	N	%
Rejection	2	8	3	14	1	13	6	11
Hurt adoptive parents	9	35	3	14	2	25	14	25
Society	5	19	3	14	0	0	8	14
Intrude on birth mother	3	12	4	18	0	0	7	13
Search results	7	27	9	41	5	63	21	38
Total	26	101	22	101	8	101	56	101

Note: This pattern of response is consistent for both genders and all age cohorts.

who gave me birth. I had to wait because she would have never understood. I didn't want to hurt her. She was too important to me' (female, age 55). This fear of disrupting their adoptive parent–child relationship contrasted with the fear of the dubious adoptee–birth mother contact that might arise from search. Six (11 per cent) of the responses fell, therefore, under the category 'fear of rejection.' This fear is understandable because the birth mother symbolically 'rejects' her birth child when she signs the relinquishment papers (Benet, 1976). Although this issue is discussed in much greater detail in the following chapters, it is a significant topic of concern for adoptees who must prepare themselves for the possibility of a 'second' rejection when they decide to search for and establish contact with their birth mothers.

The largest category (twenty-one, or 38 per cent) of responses explaining the postponement of search fell within the category 'fear of search results.' As one adoptee noted, 'I had to get prepared. I didn't know what I was going to find. I might find a prostitute or an alcoholic. A down-and-outer. Or, I might find someone who had pulled their lives together. I had to prepare myself to accept anything. Then, you can face what you get' (male, age 40). Another said, 'I had to get over the attitude that I might be opening up something that I wish I hadn't gotten myself into. I might find a real mess. I might find someone on skid row. Someone that I might have to worry about that would be a real drain on me. Not financially, you know. An unpleasant situation that I would wish that I didn't know about' (female, age 44). And another said, 'I envisioned all kinds of things. I wondered, "Is she rich?" "Is she poor?" "Is she a drunk?" I prepared myself that if she was a lonely old drunk in a room that I had to deal with that. I knew that was a possibility. Or, also someone who might cling to me for help. There are so many directions to go. She could be anything or anybody. I had to be able to accept what I got' (female, age 31).

As members of their community, these adoptees knew the social stigma carried by their birth mother and the negative labels attached to her status as a birth mother. They could not discount those images because they lacked information about their birth mother's past life and current information about her present situation. Others' reinforcement of negative birth mother stereotypes supported their fear of engaging in an undesirable contact. These adoptees had to prepare themselves, therefore, for any possible reunion outcome before they could search. Thus, one man stated, 'To say you are adopted is to also say that you are illegitimate. Now, it's different because young girls keep their babies all the time. But, before, if you said that you were illegitimate that meant something bad. To have a child and not be married was a crime. So, when you said that you wanted to search, everyone wondered why you wanted to find this terrible person. You really got the idea that you shouldn't do it' (male adoptee, age 35).

Of particular note were contacts with professionals who supported this fear by perpetuating negative stereotypes of birth mothers. For example, one long-term Parent Finders member reported a 'disapproving' social worker who worked at the adoption agency. She noted that 'there was this social worker that I had when I went to get my information. A lot of people at Parent Finders got the same kind of reaction. The first thing she said was, "Well, you know your mother wasn't married don't you?" Well, hey, we kinda of figured that one out. Usually that's why people were given up. But there was more to it. She said it as if my birth mother was a bad person or something because she wasn't married. This worker started to go into all the rotten things that I might find. When someone does something like that, you really wonder. Should I do it or not?' (female, age 41).

When these adoptees combined those negative stereotypes of birth mothers with the possible impairment of their adoptive parent–child relationship, they were suspended between their desire for reunion and their fear of the outcome of the search. The multidimensional quality of adoptees' fears about search and the uncertainty of positive outcome of contact with their birth mothers left them at an impasse. They required a more compelling motive for contact with birth mothers that would justify their search both to themselves and to others. The majority found that motive through the occurrence of a major life-change event.

Like those adoptees in other research samples, 83 per cent of these adoptees experienced a major life-change event within a six-month period before their search began (Sobol and Cardiff, 1983: 480; Sorosky et al., 1974: 204; Thompson et al., 1978: 21; Triseliotis, 1973: 174). These life-change events included 'marriage or engagement,' 'pregnancy or the birth of a child,' 'death of a significant other,' reaching the 'age of majority,' 'career advancement,' and 'medical illness' (see Table 3.5). Each of these life-crisis events produced a meaningful change in the adoptees' social status and a period of personal introspection that initiated their decision to search. Yet, all of these adoptees reported similar previous life-change events, introspective periods–and no decision to search. This finding indicated the existence of an intervening factor between a life-change event and initiation of the search that has not been discussed in the research literature.

Further analysis of the interview data revealed this intervening factor to be the influence of significant others. Significant others are individuals who take on importance to us. They are those individuals whom we desire to impress. They might be individuals who we respect, want acceptance from, fear, or with whom we identify (Charon, 1992: 72). In their discussion of their reasons for search, these adoptees mentioned at least one person who fell within the category of a significant other and who had influenced their decision to search. For example, the following woman described the impact of significant others on both her postponement of search and her ultimate decision to search. She said,

Different things would happen in my life and I would think about it. When friends teased me about being adopted, I wanted to search but I was too young. At baby showers or gatherings of people. The subject would come up and some people would be unfavourable to unwed mothers or adoption or searching. It would get me to thinking. When I had my children and they were growing up, I saw that they were all different individuals. I wondered where they got their character from. But, it was really this heart problem that spurred me on. The doctor asked me about my family history. I said that I was adopted. His response was negative. Like, 'That's not going to help me. I need this information.' My husband agreed with him. That's when I decided to do it. (female, age 48).

This woman notes some of the life-change events that may stimulate

TABLE 3.5
Adoptees' life-change event within six months of search for their birth mothers (rounded to nearest per cent) ($N = 60$)

Event	Males		Females		Total	
	N	%	N	%	N	%
Pregnancy, birth of child	2	13	12	27	14	23
Engagement/marriage	3	19	9	21	12	20
Death of loved one	0	0	9	21	9	15
Illness	2	13	6	14	8	13
Turned 18	3	19	1	2	4	7
Job change, graduation	3	19	0	0	3	5
No event	3	19	7	16	10	17
Total	16	102	44	101	60	100

an adoptee's desire for contact with the birth mother. She demonstrates also how a particular life-change event may initiate the search process. Unlike her experience with previous life-change events, this woman's heart problem gave her external support for her decision to search. By stressing her need for her missing genealogical and genetic information, her doctor gave her a more acceptable motive for the search than mere genealogical curiosity or the desire for a biological connection could provide. Her husband's additional support legitimated this new definition of the situation. In this way, this woman's perception of the acceptance of search by significant others prompted a search action that led to contact with her birth mother.

Other adoptees provided similar accounts of the association between the support of a significant other and their ultimate decision to search. For example, although the research literature reports a strong correlation between searching behaviour and 'pregnancy or childbirth' (Simpson et al., 1981; Sobol and Cardiff, 1983; Sorosky et al., 1974), the majority of the women in this study claimed postponement of search at this time because they were too busy with their family responsibilities. In contrast, those adoptees (23 per cent) who initiated a search within six months of 'pregnancy or childbirth' described the influence of significant others on their search decision. To quote one mother, 'The thing that really motivated me was when I was pregnant. Here I was carrying a baby, and I had no idea what I was passing on. Then, after he was born everybody kept talking about who he looked like. It got me thinking "Who do I look like?" So, my husband encouraged me to look. He comes from a very strong family that traces back generations. I guess he knew how I felt' (female, age 36).

Comparative scenarios arose for the life-change event of 'marriage or engagement.' One young woman replied, for instance, that, 'I began after I got married. My husband's Italian and in Italy everything is open. He couldn't see why adoption was made such a big deal of here. His family is very important to him. He just couldn't imagine not knowing where you came from. So, when I mentioned searching, he encouraged me. He babysat, paid for long-distance calls, even went to meetings' (female, age 26). In a similar fashion, a young man noted his fiancée's influence on his search decision when he stated, 'She kept asking me questions about my background and my adoption. I knew that she would marry me even if I didn't search. But, for our peace of mind – hers and mine – I did it. I thought she deserved to know if she was going to marry me. It was my responsibility to let her know what she was getting into' (male adoptee, age 24).

These examples demonstrate the way in which various life-change events emphasize adoptees' need for generational continuity through their original biological connections. These particular life-change events became associated with the decision to search, however, because they involved significant others who helped to legitimate the adoptees' desire for contact with the birth mother. This perceived support of significant others helped these adoptees confront their fears of search and take directed action to search. As one woman claimed, 'I always thought about it in the back of my mind. But I wanted some reassurance that my curiosity wasn't abnormal. Probably because it might make me appear like I was the thankless child and I always wanted to make the semblance of normalness. But, when I heard this special show on the radio about how so many others did it, I thought I could too. My ideas weren't abnormal after all. I made up my mind to do it' (female, age 23).

GENDER DIFFERENCES, LIFE-CHANGE EVENTS, AND THE DECISION TO SEARCH

In this study, more female (twelve) than male adoptees (two) reported the influence of 'pregnancy or childbirth' on their decision to search. These data support the belief that 'women have a greater proclivity to search because of their closer awareness of the biological link between generations through their own pregnancies' (Sobol and Cardiff, 1983: 482). The majority of the women in this study mentioned that their pregnancies had reminded them of the events surrounding their own conception, birth, and relinquishment. They discussed how those life-change events had raised their concern over not having genealogical and genetic information to give their children. They observed also how these life-change events had made them think of their birth mothers' situation and the emotions encountered by her through relinquishment. Yet, as previously noted, the biological event of pregnancy or childbirth was not, by itself, a strong determining factor in the decision to search. Without the support of significant others, the majority of the female adoptees in this study had postponed their search at this time.

In addition to the perceived support of significant others, those female adoptees who linked 'pregnancy or childbirth' to their decision to search noted an association between these life-change events, their adoptive status, and their idealized performance of the 'mother' role. For example, one woman reported that, 'the thing that really motivated me to search was when I was pregnant with my oldest child. I realized that I was bringing a life into the world, and I had no medical information. My parents wouldn't give it to me because they didn't have it either. All of a sudden, I started to worry about whether I had anything hereditary that would affect the baby. I might be giving something to my baby that I didn't even know about. I felt responsible' (female adoptee, age 39). Another said, 'When my son was a baby, he had to go to Sick Kids to get all these tests. When they asked for background information, and I obviously don't have any because I am adopted, they wrote "Mother Adopted" in big red letters across the front of his file. It really bothered me. I felt that my kid was being labelled because of me' (female adoptee, age 38).

Women are the primary caregivers and the chief agents of procreation in our patriarchal society (Levine and Estable, 1990: 8). Because women's worth is defined with reference to these 'mothering' functions, they gain considerable status and prestige through their satisfactory performance of the 'mother' role (Caplan, 1989; Levine and Estable, 1990; Rich, 1986). The idealized image of 'mother' is, however, impossible to meet. As mothers, women are expected to be self-sacrificing, all-giving, constantly present, and continually supportive (Rich, 1986: 115). 'Good' mothers are 'endless founts of nurturance, naturally know how to raise their children, and never get angry' (Caplan, 1989: 70). When women fall short of this idealized image, they are labelled 'bad' or 'inadequate'. For this reason, most women experience feelings of personal failure in their role as 'mothers' (Rossiter, 1988: 5). Female adoptees are disadvantaged further in that role performance because they lack the genetic information necessary for their children's physical health and well-being.

Those women who reported the influence of 'pregnancy or childbirth' on their decision to search noted, in particular, how their adoptive status damaged their idealized performance of the mother role. They mentioned also the social discrimination imposed on their children for this 'personal failing' (Goffman, 1963: 9). In these ways, the life-change event of 'pregnancy or childbirth' produced major consequences for these adoptees' view of self as 'good' mothers. Search offered them a way to improve their role performance and gain more satisfactory presentations of self which would, in turn, affirm their personal identity.

In contrast, many of the male adoptees in this study listed 'occupational or career' advancement (three or 19 per cent) and 'age of majority' status (three or 19 per cent) as life-change events occurring within six months prior to search. Because men experience more opportunities to gain feelings of self-worth and personal achievement through their position in the paid labour force, life-change events in those areas are more likely to stimulate their desire for reunion. Genealogical and genetic information is linked more strongly, however, to family concerns and family structure than to issues arising in the paid labour force. Thus, male adoptees may find their adoptive status less threatening to their personal identity because it is likely to arise less frequently to discount their satisfactory presentation of self. They may be less compelled, therefore, to achieve contact with their birth mothers.

Women, however, spend considerable time involved in family functions performing family roles (Fox, 1993; Nett, 1993). Their labour and, consequently, many feelings of self-worth are formed primarily within that domain. For example, the majority of the social events avoided by the adoptees in this study centred around such family functions as baby showers, wedding showers or christenings. These social functions are attended mainly by women. Thus, women, who live primarily within the social world of family and family connections, may encounter more social stigma through adoption than do their male counterparts and more opportunity for support by significant others. This social factor may account for the large proportion of female searchers found in the research literature.

The category 'death of a family member' demonstrates the investment made by female adoptees in their family roles. All of the adoptees in this study who reported the 'death of a family member' as a life-change event were female (nine or 15 per cent). In four of those cases, the 'death of a family member' involved the death of an adoptive parent. Those four women had viewed search as a threat to their adoptive parent–child relationship and harmful to their idealized role performance of 'devoted daughter'. One of these women replied, 'It's always something in the back of your mind. But, you don't want to do it because of your parents. You know that your mother doesn't really care for that to happen. So, it was after she died that I really felt free to do it. Because, then, there would be no way that she could ever be hurt by it' (female, age 65). In another instance, a young woman searched to maintain her role of 'sister' through a possible relationship with biological siblings. She said, 'I started my search after my brother had been killed in an accident. I was aching for a family relationship. I needed a brother. Not someone who was going to wrap their arms around me. I needed to know that I still had family somewhere. A brother or sister maybe. Someone that I was related to. Even though he was four years younger and his biological parents are my adoptive parents, I missed him a lot. I guess that I was looking for a replacement' (female, age 38). In this way, these life-change events emphasized the full implications of non-disclosure for these adoptees' personal identity, the organization of their social world, and the satisfactory performance of other roles that were more central to their personal identity.

Goffman (1963) describes a stigmatization process in which individuals encounter discrimination from others who question their social identity. This chapter outlines a similar process for adoptees who experience non-disclosure. Adoption stigmatizes adoptees when it severs their original kinship ties. Secrecy emphasizes that social stigma when it produces biographical discontinuities that discredit adoptees' presentation of self. Adoptees reflect upon others' reactions to those presentations and incorporate them as part of their personal identity. In this way, adoptees may perceive themselves as personally flawed through adoption.

The sixty reunited adoptees in this study viewed their adoptive status as social stigma. They supported that view with specific examples of social discrimination by others who questioned their social identity. That discrimination process emphasized the possibility of a 'real' birth identity based on their genetic and genealogical background and raised personal doubts about the adoptive identity created within the adoptive family structure. This factor explains the feelings of personal uncertainty and apprehension reported by adoptees who seek contact with their birth mother. It explains also the diverse social, emotional, and psychological characteristics of searchers and the wide range of interest in reunion expressed by the adopted population. Based on these reports, the strength of adoptees' desire for contact with their birth mother is associated strongly with their social experience as 'adoptees' and the significant value placed by others on their missing blood ties.

The impact of others' opinions is seen in the decision-making process involved in the search. As members of their community, adoptees know the legal and social constraints on search for and contact with birth mothers. Their reasons for postponement of the search reflect those social sanctions. Their fear of hurting their adoptive parents or of finding undesirable birth mothers demonstrates how they had internalized the messages of non-disclosure. These adoptees needed a stronger justification for reunion than genealogical curiosity before they could search.

That search catalyst took the form of a life-change event. These life-change events created periods of self-reflection in which these adoptees considered the implications of their adoptive status. At that time, significant others helped them confront their search fears and make a decision to search. The strong association between these life-change events and unsatisfactory enactments of other, more significant role performances contributed to that decision-making process.

The association between life-change events and the initiation of the search revealed a strong gender distinction in the decision to search. The women in this study were affected more by such life-change events as marriage or pregnancy than were the men – who were influenced by such changes as career status. Because one's genealogical and genetic background is likely to be drawn more frequently into interactions involving family issues, female adoptees are more likely to have their major role performances discredited than are men who exist mainly in a different social world. This social factor helps explain the larger number of female adoptees who express interest in contact with their birth mother and the predominance of female adoptees in the research literature.

4

The Search

The previous chapter describes the effects of non-disclosure on adoptees' personal and social identities. This chapter outlines the effects of the search. The search involves a series of stages in which adoptees locate pieces of their genealogical and genetic background and link them together to discover their birth mother's identity. Those stages include: (1) contact with a search agency, (2) gaining access to the birth mother's surname, (3) confronting a birth identity, (4) getting non-identifying background information, (5) obsession with the search, and (6) identification of the birth mother. Each stage produces introspective periods over the significance of adoption, search, and contact with the birth mother on the adoptees' view of self. Each additional stage creates a stronger commitment to contact with the birth mother and satisfactory outcome of the reunion.

CONTACT WITH SEARCH AGENCIES

Once adoptees confront the fear and uncertainty involved in the decision-making stage of the search, 'the next step is to call the court, the adoption agency or a search organization for search assistance' (Gonyo and Watson, 1988: 19). The adoptees in this study contacted Parent Finders. During that first telephone call, they spoke to a volunteer member who validated their search and reunion concerns. They heard about the legal restrictions of non-disclosure and the organization's activism for an open record system. They learned about the group's dedication to the search and the outcome of contact with birth mothers. That contact call led these adoptees to a Parent Finders meeting, where they received individual assistance with their searches.

At Parent Finders meetings, these adoptees found a group of 'sympathetic others' who confirmed their perception of self, their search goals, and their desire for contact with their birth mothers (Goffman, 1963: 19). For the majority, this meeting was their first experience with an open awareness context in which others fully accepted their adoptive identity. They reported that, 'It was really easy to talk in the group because everybody was adopted. If I said something about adoption they would understand. For example, when I found out my birth name, I called my husband and told him. He was happy for me. But, when I called my Parent Finders friend, she knew exactly how I felt. Like, it was earth shattering! It wasn't just nice. She was so excited for me. She just didn't take it calmly. There was a natural communication between us' (female, age 39). This mutual understanding between Parent Finders members helped these adoptees accept their background information and integrate it more easily as a part of self. It gave them a safe place to express their concerns about the search and their desires for contact with their birth mothers openly without fear of individual criticism or social censure. Together, Parent Finders members shared their social status as adoptees who suffered the effects of non-disclosure.

Parent Finders meetings concentrate on issues of search for and contact with birth mothers. The formal section of the meeting presents search stories by recently reunited members, legal issues involved in the search, and newly discovered search tactics. Volunteers help with individual search questions after the formal section of the meeting ends. During this informal period, group members discuss their adoption, their search progress, and their early reunion experience with other members. They offer suggestions and emotional support. Many members form friendships and meet between the monthly meetings. In this way, continued attendance at Parent Finders meetings strengthens the adoptees' commitment to search and their dedication to contact with the birth mother.

Watching the slow but steady progress of others in various stages of search and early contact with birth mothers socializes new members into the role of 'searcher.' Other members' technical assistance and emotional support contributes to an easy acceptance of that role. Members welcome each new piece of disclosed information as a group triumph. They greet each individual setback as a group disappointment. This close identification with other members' experience of search for and contact with birth mothers produces hope for one's own reunion. In this way, the common bond of adoption unites members to achieve the collective goal of reunion for all Parent Finders searchers. As one woman who encountered a seven-year search explained, 'There were people getting reunions. I wasn't getting anywhere. It was really hard. But it was good to see some find who they wanted. I just kept going. Just in case something did happen. If I was around, then, I would be there for it. Which is what happened. A member went one of the extreme routes to help me and got the answer' (female, age 41). To give up the search means failing the group as well as oneself.

GAINING ACCESS TO THE BIRTH MOTHER'S SURNAME

The next step in the search involves knowledge of the birth mother's surname at the time of her relinquishment. Because their original birth records are sealed, adoptees possess birth certificates containing their adoptive names. In Ontario before 1968, the birth mother's surname was written on the adoption order given to the adoptive parents. Adoption orders produced after 1968 have serial numbers in place of that surname. Those adoptees must register, therefore, with the Ontario Adoption Disclosure Register, which will search for them. At present there are almost 9,000 adoptees on the register's list waiting for its three employees to access their birth mother's name (*Ottawa Citizen*, 16 December 1993: C3). Although many of those adoptees continue to search through self-help organizations like Parent Finders, they experience limited success without this piece of identifiable information. The length of this stage of the search depends, therefore, upon the availability of the birth mother's surname on legal documents connected to birth, relinquishment, or adoption.

Adoptees born before 1968 may conduct their own search with the use of the birth mother's surname on the adoption order. The majority of adoptees react strongly, however, when they learn about the adoption order at their first Parent Finders meeting. Once again, they must confront their fear over the possible disruption by the search of their adoptive parent–child relationship. Some get angry, say their search is impossible, leave the meeting, and never return. Others obtain the name from sympathetic relatives, family friends, doctors, or lawyers who had become aware through other circumstances of the birth mother's surname. Some remember the name from childhood when they found their adoption order 'snooping through my parents' things.' The remainder ask their adoptive parents directly.

The decision over how to gain access to the birth mother's surname requires careful deliberation that may delay the search considerably. The major consideration in this decision-making process is the possible reaction of the adoptive parents to the request for the adoption order. Of the sixty adoptees interviewed for this study, twelve (20 per cent) postponed their search until after their adoptive parents' deaths, when they acquired their adoption order with other legal papers (see Table 4.1). Fourteen (23 per cent) remembered the name from childhood, asked a sympathetic other for assistance, or searched their parents' home secretly for the papers. These adoptees explained their avoidance of an open request for the adoption order as a way to protect their parents from the emotional distress caused by knowledge of their child's desire for contact with their birth mother. Yet, their actions also protected self. One of these adoptees had perceived that 'whenever the subject of adoption came up, which wasn't very often, they would say how much they wanted me. They made it quite plain that there wasn't going to be any information exchanged. My mother likes to think of me as hers. She would have seen it as a rejection in some way. She'd sit up all night thinking, "What did I do wrong? Where have I failed." I could just see that happen. So, I never asked for any papers. I never mentioned the subject at all. I got the name from someone else' (male, age 35).

These 'avoidant' searchers believed their parents would be hurt by their searching behaviour. That belief was supported by the pretence awareness contexts established previously by their parents whenever the topic of their adoption arose. Thus, these adoptees could not share their concerns about reunion with their parents, because they had been taught not to bring their full identity to interactions involving the topic of adoption, search, or contact with birth mothers. To protect the primacy of their adoptive parent–child relationship, they used the interaction rules established by their parents and pretended no desire to search for and no desire to contact their birth mother.

The remaining adoptees (thirty-four or 57 per cent) asked their parents for their adoption order. Only six (10 per cent) received their parents' positive support for this request. Nineteen (32 per cent) reported underlying feelings of distress from their parents when they asked for the adoption order. Seven of those nineteen adoptees used the open awareness context created by their request for their adoption order to discuss their parents' concerns about contact with the birth mother. One of them explained that 'I had to tell my parents. I had never kept anything from them. This was something important. I don't think that it was fair to keep it away from them. But, my adoptive mother was very threatened. I tried to explain to her that at my age you don't run away from home. I was married and had two kids. She thought that I was looking for another mother. I had to convince her that I wasn't. We talk about it. So, she is getting better. She has a hard time understanding that I searched for me. It has nothing to do with her' (female, age 39).

Although a difficult procedure, this open awareness context produced continued discussions about adoption, search, and reunion that drew parent and child closer together. In this way, these 'open' adoptees gained a stronger

TABLE 4.1
Response of adoptive parents to adoptees' request for adoption order
(rounded to nearest per cent) ($N = 60$)

Parents' response	N	%
Deceased	12	20
Did not tell	14	23
Angry	9	15
Sad, hurt	19	32
Supportive	6	10
Total	60	100

Note: There was no significant difference in response on the basis of gender.

understanding of their parents' position in the adoption triangle. Although reluctant at first, the parent also began to perceive the search as an issue of identity rather than a threat to their parent–child relationship. One woman noted, for example, that 'Being so open about it helped me understand my mother. I never thought of the pain that she felt not having children and maybe of losing me. One day I told her that it was nice to finally meet someone who looked like me. She told me that she knew how I felt because she had always felt close to my cousins because they resembled her. I never thought how hard it was for her not to have children of her own. To see herself in her own children like that' (female, age 19). Another remarked, 'My dad was really shocked. We've become closer for it. It was the first time in my life that I found out how he really felt about me. He was really scared of losing me. All of a sudden, I knew how much my parents cared about me. It was good to talk about it' (female, age 31).

The remaining adoptees (twelve of the nineteen) pretended to give up the idea of search. Like the 'avoidant' adoptees, these adoptees had worried about the effects of search on their adoptive parent–child relationship but could not obtain a birth name without an adoption order request. Their parents' obvious distress at their request for their adoption orders confirmed their concern. To alleviate further distress for their parents, they pretended to give up the idea of a search. Their parents contributed to this pretence awareness context by never discussing the subject with them again. In this way, both parties protected their adoptive parent–child relationship by ignoring the stress that contact with the birth mother might produce. To quote one woman, 'My mom came out of the bedroom with the order and she said, "This is your mother's name." I thought that was so funny coming from her. I said, "Hey, you're my mom." But I knew I had hurt her. So,

I kept on searching and I didn't tell them. They don't ask and I don't say anything at all. I never want to hurt her like that again' (female, age 29).

The last group (nine or 15 per cent) encountered extreme hostility from their parents when they requested a copy of the adoption order. This group had expected this angry reaction and had avoided asking for the adoption order until all other alternatives had been explored. As a member of this group explained, 'When I originally didn't want to ask for my adoption order, it was self-preservation. I knew what kind of a scene there would be. I wanted to avoid it at all costs. I kept going to meetings and trying to search. I finally had to ask. I couldn't do my search without it. My mother was livid. She said there was no such document. I kept insisting. Then, she said, "You'll get it over my dead body." It caused quite a rift between us. She never forgave me' (female, age 40).

To protect their adoptive parent–child relationship and alleviate their parents' anger towards them, this group also abandoned their request for the adoption order and engaged in pretence awareness contexts with their parents. As a result of this action, this group experienced very long searches and used drastic measures to learn the identity of the birth mother. For example, one woman learned her birth name after she called every hospital in the city where she was born and asked about all of the babies delivered on her birth date. Another woman found her birth mother when she telephoned a local radio show and asked the listening audience for search assistance. These radical search tactics emphasize the determination and ability of searching adoptees to overcome any barrier in their effort to learn further genetic and genealogical background information that will lead to identification of the birth mother.

From these examples one can see that, once these adoptees committed themselves to search, they committed themselves to its completion. Few were willing, however, to jeopardize their adoptive parent–child relationship to achieve contact with the birth mother. The majority of the adoptees in this study raised this concern initially when they explained their reasons for postponement of the search. They recognized their parents' fear over the possible loss of their children to an unknown birth mother. Their parents' reaction to their request for their adoption order supported this perception. To avoid further distress for their parents and to protect this significant relationship the majority of these adoptees pretended to have little interest in the search. Yet, as the 'open' adoptees in this study noted, revelation of their desire for reunion may strengthen – rather than weaken – the adoptive parent–child bond. By surrounding these interactions within pretence awareness contexts, adoptees eliminate the opportunity to share this major life-change event with their parents. Because neither party brings their full identity to the interaction process, they curtail the personal growth that may emerge as both parent and child support each other through search and contact with the birth mother.

CONFRONTING A BIRTH IDENTITY

Few adoptees know about their adoption order before they come to Parent Finders. Most are surprised, then, to learn also of their own birth names. These birth names confirm the existence of a birth identity. That birth identity validates their biological connection to the birth mother and confirms the events surrounding their conception, birth, and relinquishment. For example, upon discussing her birth name, one woman remarked that 'it never occurred to me that I would have another name. I was intrigued when I saw it. I guess that my parents convinced me I was a total non-entity when I came into their life. I never thought that I had been named or anything. I thought my existence began the day that they came to get me' (female, age 36).

These birth names provide the first tangible evidence of a 'birth' identity separate from the 'adoptive' identity formed within the adoptive family structure. Some adoptees require time, therefore, to consider the implications of that other identity and absorb it as a part of self. For example, one woman observed that 'When I saw the name, it was really weird. I thought, "This is me!" The more that I looked at that document, the stranger it got. I knew that is was me that they were talking about. I thought, "It's me. No, it's not me. But, it's me." I kept going back and forth. I stuffed it away in the bottom of my drawer. I forgot about it for a few more years until I felt ready to search' (female, age 37).

The process of accepting the birth name as a part of self may take only a few moments or many years. No one can predict how any adoptee will react to any particular piece of background information. The search may stop or be delayed, therefore, at any stage while adoptees deliberate over their findings and absorb their newly discovered genealogical background as a part of self. In this way, the ability of searching adoptees to accept their birth identity affects the search process as much as their ease of access to their background information. Until they accept this new view of self, they cannot continue the search and establish contact with the birth mother.

Acceptance of the birth identity as a part of self is a difficult process to describe. As soon as adoptees are told of their adoption, they become aware of the existence of another identity that operates as a hidden part of self. Because they have speculated for years about the characteristics of that birth identity, the majority accept their background information with composure. Just as they need to face the full range of possible birth mother contacts before they initiate the search, they must confront the full range of likely birth identities for self. As a long-term Parent Finders member explained, 'Everybody has their own nemesis. I've helped people where it was a case of incest. They handled it. I found a retarded mother in a mental hospital. The adoptee worked through it. I had one adoptee who was absolutely distraught to find his parents were university students who relinquished him so they could continue their education. He never forgave them. What is hard for me may be nothing to you. If you think that maybe you're not ready, then, maybe you should back off until you are. That is the whole point of controlling your own search. That is why we try not to push but let adoptees take each stage of search at their own leisure' (female, age 42).

Few adoptees at Parent Finders meetings reacted negatively to knowledge of their birth name. Most had prepared themselves for the prospect of a birth identity during the decision-making process involved in the search and through others' curiosity about their biological background. Their contact with other searchers at Parent Finders helped them also through this transition process. One woman described this process as 'shocking but nice. At my first meeting, somebody said to me, "What was your name?" I thought she meant my adoptive name and I told her. She said, "No, your birth name." I said, "Oh, I don't have one." I really didn't believe it. I thought they had just given me a number in the hospital nursery and later my parents were kind enough to give me a name. I was too poor for one of my own. It was so hard to take in that I had a name of my own because I thought that I was just a number. It helped when they explained it. When I finally got that name, I was excited' (female, age 42). By the time this woman learned her birth name, she was looking for it with anticipation and welcomed it as an important source of information about herself.

APPLICATION FOR NON-IDENTIFYING INFORMATION

The next stage of the search involves an application to the adoption agency for non-identifying background information. Non-identifying information consists of background material that cannot be linked directly to the identity of the birth parents' (Sachdev, 1989: 89). It includes both birth parents' physical descriptions, their levels of education, marital status, number of siblings, occupation, personal interests, and hobbies. In contrast, medical information contains information on hereditary characteristics, diseases, and disabilities of both birth parents and their families (Sachdev, 1989: 89). Some medical information includes details on the birth mother's pregnancy or delivery and the early medical history of the adoptee. Adoptees often apply for their medical information first, as those requests may be received more sympathetically (Gonyo and Watson, 1988: 19). Then they use their request for medical information as an entry to their non-identifying information.

Considerable variation exists in the type and amount of medical or background information released. Depending upon agency policy, the worker who composes the background material for release, and the amount of information obtained originally from the birth mother, adoptees may receive two lines or five pages. Whatever the amount, this background material provides unknown details about self. Thus, despite its superficial content, the arrival of background material elicits considerable emotion. For instance, one young woman replied, 'I ripped the envelope open. I was very excited. It was incredible! I thought, "God, I'm Irish!" I didn't know what I was. I had been told things by my parents but you never know for sure. Here was five pages about myself. I thought. "This is great!" I cried. Because, I had finally got it. I called my friend. She wasn't that interested. I thought, "How could she not want to know? It's me!" I was going crazy. It was wonderful to learn about me' (female, age 26).

Many agencies require a personal interview before they release non-identifying information to adoptees. Those adoptees in this study (sixteen or 26 per cent) who attended such interviews engaged in suspicion awareness contexts in which only the agency worker knew their birth identity. That interaction context was extremely difficult for these adoptees because it emphasized their powerless status as individuals who lacked control over intimate details about self. For example, one woman remarked, 'I walked into the room. The worker said, "Oh, I thought you would have red hair." I was shocked. I asked her why she had said that. She said, "Your mother was a redhead." You could have knocked me over with a feather. Because this person who I knew absolutely nothing about had red hair. I could see it in my mind. It was a strange experience to hear this. And, the other things that I didn't know anything about. I got the usual background sheet with the number of siblings, her age, her occupation, her interests. I knew nothing of this. I was dumbfounded' (female, age 44).

This suspicion awareness context reinforced these adoptees' perception of adoption as social stigma. The agency worker knew their birth identity. However, as adoptees, they were not allowed access to that identity. In addition, the agency worker possessed the power to dictate the type and the amount of information they would receive. This situation increased their determination to establish contact with the birth mother. One replied, 'I sat there. Here I was at age thirty-eight and she had control over what I was allowed to see about myself. I felt like I was going to rip the piece of paper out of her hand and strangle her! How dare she just sit there and read it but not read it to me! Then, when she started to read things off, it didn't match what my parents had told me. I made her go check to see if she had the right information. I was right, she did have someone else's file. I decided I had to find my birth mother. No one could give me the wrong information again. I would know myself' (female, age 42). Another said, 'It bothered me a lot not to have that information. It made me really angry. You or this person downtown or anyone can come in and look at my file and know everything about me but I can't. Who are those records being kept for anyway if not for the adoptee! Who really cares about that information except me? What's it to them? That made it all the more imperative to find my birth mother and all the more joyful when we met. Because when I found her I could get all my questions answered' (female, age 20).

These two quotes describe the two major emotions involved in the search process. One is the excitement attached to the power of learning about self. The other is the anger attached to the powerless position created by non-disclosure. These two emotions increase adoptees' desire for contact with the birth mother. As the search continues, the closed awareness context surrounding interactions involving their genetic and genealogical background begins to change into a more open awareness context. Access to more background information removes more biographical discontinuities. To eliminate their biographical discontinuities completely, they require contact with the one person who was present during their conception, birth, and relinquishment. In this way, the birth mother becomes the prime objective of their search. When adoptees learn the birth mother's identity, they gain access to a resource person who can inform them of all of the missing events in their early biography.

OBSESSION WITH THE SEARCH

Once adoptees have their non-identifying information, they match it with the birth mother's surname. Then they check this material against public data available in city directories, court records, historical town documents, cemetery plots, church baptismal records, newspaper files, school yearbooks, and so forth until they identify the birth mother's current address. The length of this stage of the search depends upon the type of background information received and the unique character of the birth family surname. Some searches may last for only a few hours, while others take several years. Adoptees' obsession with the search drives them, however, to finish this stage of the search as quickly as possible. The more information obtained, the more they want to learn the birth mother's identity. The more that they learn about her identity, the more committed they become to contact with her.

Over half (thirty-eight or 64 per cent) of the adoptees in this study discovered their birth mother's identity within a twenty-four-hour period after they matched their non-identifying information with her surname. Fourteen (23 per cent) completed their search within a week (see Table 4.2). These adoptees attributed the speed of their search to an escalating desire for more genetic and genealogical information about self. They had experienced the sense of personal power produced when they received their non-identifying background information. Given a small taste, they wanted more. In this way, 'the search became an obsession. Even though I didn't expect to get so involved. It kind of took me over. I just ignored everything for about eight weeks. My husband looked after things while I ignored everybody. I was so absorbed' (female, age 39).

This obsession with the search escalated as the search continued and these adoptees gathered more and more background material. Each time they uncovered a new piece of information, they tested its appropriateness and added it to previous pieces. Each time another piece of information was revealed, the closer they were to completion of the search. The closer they were to completion of the search, the greater the intensity of their desire to search. The search represented 'a kind of puzzle. It was extremely interesting. I was finding out about all of these people and placing them together and connecting them into a total picture in which I was also a part. I became more excited as each piece of information was gained. Putting it all together to tell a whole story. I was high all the time' (female, age 49).

Yet this puzzle was not an ordinary puzzle. Finding the solution to this puzzle meant gaining the answer to the question, 'Who am I?' When these adoptees linked together the missing pieces of their genealogical and genetic background, they placed themselves within the same biosocial context in which others in their community existed. As they deciphered the mysterious events surrounding their conception, birth, and relinquishment, they also eliminated the biographical inconsistencies produced by non-disclosure. Thus, the solution to this puzzle presented these adoptees with the ability

TABLE 4.2
Length of adoptees' search before identification of birth mother (rounded to nearest per cent)
($N = 60$)

Length of search	Males		Females		Total	
	N	%	N	%	N	%
Under 24 hours	4	25	5	11	9	15
Under a week	4	25	10	23	14	23
1 week to 1 month	2	13	4	9	6	10
2 to 6 months	3	19	6	14	9	15
7 to 11 months	1	6	6	14	7	12
12 to 23 months	2	13	6	14	8	13
2 to 5 years	0	0	5	11	5	8
Over 5 years	0	0	2	5	2	3
Total	16	101	44	101	60	101

to be like the remainder of their community, that is, like 'normals' (Goffman, 1963). It gave them, what one adoptee described as 'that part of myself that I didn't know. My beginning. It's so elemental but when you are adopted, you sometimes feel like you were hatched. There is no information about that aspect of your life. It's mystifying. I was getting answers! About what. Who. How it all happened. How it all came about. Like, I have a beginning and I know that I'll have an end! I wasn't hatched!' (female, age 33).

The excitement created by this discovery of unknown parts of self produced a stronger interest in the birth mother's identity. The birth mother symbolized the adoptees' biological connection to others. She held intimate knowledge of the events surrounding their conception, birth, and relinquishment. Thus, during this particular stage of the search, those adoptees who had resisted the idea of reunion found themselves also desiring contact with the birth mother. One, therefore, claimed that 'I was one of the adoptees who always said, "Why would you want to do it?" These people who raised you are your family. But it was really funny. When I decided to do it, I almost went crazy to have it done. It had to be done quickly. Not for the surgery, which was the reason that I started. For me! Once I got started on it, I couldn't quit. I got very involved in it. Almost like an obsession. I had to find her' (female, age 30).

This obsession with the search led many adoptees to use extreme search tactics to verify the identity of the birth mother. For example, many approached previous neighbours, co-workers, or schoolmates of birth family members for more background information on the birth mother and possible clues about her present life. These adoptees disguised their search by saying that they were completing a family tree on people who carried the birth surname or that they were trying to find this person to participate in a family, work, or school reunion event. This obsession with the search placed both their own and their birth mother's confidentiality at risk. For instance, during one of these 'fishing' calls to a birth uncle, the birth mother was visiting his home and he called her to the telephone to speak to the adoptee. In a state of shock, the adoptee revealed her identity to the birth mother, was acknowledged, and then a week later received a letter from the birth mother asking to be left alone. This woman believed her birth mother had rejected her because she had broken confidentiality during this telephone call.

It was not unusual, then, for adoptees to spend hundreds of dollars on long-distance telephone calls to other cities to speak with someone who might have background information, or to ask friends to examine church or municipal records during a vacation trip. Once the search began, these searchers took every possible step to learn and verify the birth mother's identity. Although they laid the search aside for short periods to meet the demands of other aspects of their lives that needed attention, their obsession with the search predominated. Disappointments over the refusal of others to release background material became short term as new search plans or strategies arose to overcome them so they could achieve their ultimate search goal, that is, learning the birth mother's identity.

Obsession with the search may energize the search and speed up its completion, but it also causes searchers often to lose perspective on their actions. Thus many adoptees with limited background material or such common surnames as 'Smith' or 'Brown' used unorthodox routes to learn the identity of the birth mother. One woman became employed, for instance, in the records department of a hospital and searched for her birth records during her coffee breaks and lunch hours. Another woman examined old university yearbook pictures trying to match her picture with the physical characteristics of previous graduates. A third went to the birth family's former neighbourhood and asked all of the older shopkeepers if they remembered the birth mother.

In retrospect, during the interview schedule, several of these adoptees regretted their impulsive behaviour and their lack of discretion during the search. They described themselves as 'so crazy,' 'on such a terrific high,' or 'so out of control' that they were not making sensible decisions. Their search had put them on a roller-coaster ride of extreme emotion. The sense of power gained through their new-found knowledge of self had combined with their anger over non-disclosure to make them lose perspective on the search. One woman said, 'I was so obsessed that I can't believe it. Like, you'd have to be nuts to do this. The family name was German. I had this map of Germany. If you phone person-to-person, you don't have to pay. I phoned as many people with my birth name as I could. All over Germany! I mean, I must have made hundreds of calls trying to find her. I felt that it was my only hope. You know, no one knows anything but maybe this guy does. It was like finding a needle in a haystack. That's how crazy it got. It was an obsession. Stupid things like that. Now, I think that it was stupid. At the time, I didn't care. I would have done anything to find out' (female, age 23). Regardless of the cost or consequences, these adoptees were determined to find their birth mothers.

IDENTIFICATION OF THE BIRTH MOTHER

Obsession with the search ends when adoptees verify the birth mother's current address. Once identified, the birth mother is no longer an abstract entity. She becomes a real person. When adoptees discover her address, contact with the birth mother becomes possible. At this point, searchers face the decision of whether to contact the birth mother and request a meeting. This decision-making process requires a new commitment of self to the search and contact with the birth mother. Thus, a young woman noted that 'When I found her, then, she became a real person. I put the brakes on. I began to realize what I was doing. What it was going to be like for that person. For you to walk into her life after thirty years. She obviously had not wanted to find me or she would have searched. I had to think about whether I wanted to disrupt her life. Finally, I decided that if I was going to do it, then, I had to do it' (female, age 30).

The decision-making process involved in contact with the birth mother provides the link between search and reunion. It represents the turning-point where the shelter of non-disclosure disappears and confidentiality ends. When adoptees establish contact with the birth mother, they make the birth mother an active participant in the reunion process. When they reveal their own identity to her, they open the door for her also to enter their life. They must consider the risks involved for them, therefore, before they contact her.

At this point, the support of others becomes paramount. Yet, obsession with the search frequently isolates adoptees from significant others who are not engaged in the search process. In addition, although the majority of these adoptees claimed support from their husbands, their children, close friends, and other family members, they sensed a lack of understanding of the need to search and gain contact with the birth mother. Family and friends did not demonstrate enough excitement when new background information was uncovered. They were not as disappointed or depressed when background material was denied or not available. As one woman claimed 'my family supported me as best as they could. But, like others, they don't really understand. When I came home with my background information, they tried to appear excited for me. But, they really couldn't understand what all the excitement was about. Especially, my husband. He is not close to his family. He jokes sometimes about why do I want to go looking when he'd be happy to lose some of the ones he's got' (female, age 42). Although these close intimates wanted to help, they did not comprehend the full meaning of this knowledge for the adoptee's identity.

In contrast, other adoptees at Parent Finders meetings possessed an instant understanding of the identity issues produced by non-disclosure. These adoptees turned increasingly, therefore, to other Parent Finder members as their search progressed. The open awareness context available at Parent Finders gave them a safe environment for the expression of their concerns. Other Parent Finders members' acceptance and understanding of their adoptive identity supported that process. In addition, the group offered contact intermediaries, advice on different contact techniques, and examples of reactions of birth mothers to contact. Members of the organization helped these adoptees with the intense emotions produced by verification of the birth mother's present identity and the idea of a meeting with the birth mother. In this way, Parent Finders members experience an emotional commitment to the search and positive support during the process of self-absorption needed to assimilate their background information as a part of self.

The search is an intimate act. It considers that part of self denied to adoptees through non-disclosure. By gaining access to their genealogical and genetic background, searching adoptees neutralize their sense of being different through adoption. Each new piece of background material removes the doubts about personal identity formed by the adoptees' biographical discontinuities. Each new piece of information on the birth mother verifies the biological connection demanded by others. In this way, searching adoptees attempt to 'normalize' self and remove the social stigma caused by their adoptive status (Goffman, 1963: 6).

The search progresses through a series of stages. These include: (1) contact with a search agency, (2) gaining access to the birth mother's surname, (3) confronting a birth identity, (4) getting non-identifying background information, (5) obsession with the search, and (6) identification of the birth mother. For the purpose of clarification, these stages have been outlined separately in this chapter. Like most social processes, however, they exhibit artificial boundaries and do not proceed always as expected. This chapter describes the typical search path. Upon making a decision to search, each adoptee enters his or her own journey of self-discovery which follows its own individual course. Some adoptees may receive their background material before they learn the birth mother's surname. Some may receive both together. Some may have been raised with knowledge of their birth name, while others have never possessed a single piece of background information before the search. Some may find that, upon a request for an adoption order, their adoptive parents arrange a contact meeting because they know the identity of the birth mother. Others may search for years to find the birth mother deceased. In this way, each search becomes an individual experience guided by the social constraints produced by non-disclosure.

Once the decision to search is made, obsession with the search drives adoptees to complete it. The continuous accumulation of previously unknown information about self produces a period of self-absorption that increases the desire to end the search and verify the birth mother's identity. This obsession with the search demands the tolerance of significant others, who may take on responsibilities that free adoptees to search and who try to respond to the adoptees' search needs. The ability of those significant others to support this obsession with the search varies, however, with their own view of family and the significance of genetic and genealogical background for completion of identity.

Parent Finders' technical guidance and emotional support is a primary resource. The group provides an open awareness context that recognizes the adoptive identity. This atmosphere of total acceptance lets adoptees express their concerns about search and reunion spontaneously without fear of social censure. With the support of the group, many adoptees continue their search through periods of dormancy when further information is not forthcoming. Others accept their background information more easily through their strong identification with others who search. At Parent Finders, each adoptee receives validation for his or her decision to search and continued support as he or she progresses through the search stages.

The search stops when adoptees learn the birth mother's current address. At this point, adoptees must decide whether they will contact the birth mother to arrange a meeting. Three major themes emerge during this decision-making process. They are: (1) fear of rejection, (2) possible interference in the birth mother's life, and (3) the primacy of the adoptive parent–child relationship. These three themes resemble the fears about the search expressed by these adoptees during their postponement of the search. They arise again to influence the dynamics of contact with the birth mother and satisfaction with that contact outcome. Analysis of these three themes is essential in the discussion of any study on the search, contact with the birth mother, and satisfaction with the outcome ofcontact. They appear as central factors, therefore, in the following chapters of this study.

5

Contact with the Birth Mother

The search ends when adoptees verify the birth mother's identity. The next stage is contact with the birth mother. Once contacted, the birth mother becomes an active participant in the outcome of the reunion. The anxiety experienced by these adoptees during their decision over contact with the birth mother demonstrates their awareness of this fact. That anxiety increased when they considered the birth mother's position in the adoption triangle. Their perception of that position influenced both the type of contact initiated with the birth mother and their submissive acceptance of her response to this contact.

These adoptees described three types of contact based on the birth mother's response to them. These were (1) discontinuation of contact by the birth mother, (2) discontinuation of contact by the adoptee, and (3) continued contact. Control over the outcome of the contact rested mainly with the birth mother. Few of these adoptees asked her for an account of her decision about contact but assigned their own explanation to her contact response. They based those explanations on their perception of the birth mother and the stigmatized status held by birth mothers because of their relinquishment.

DECISION TO MAKE CONTACT

The reunion process cannot begin until contact with birth relatives occurs (Gonyo and Watson, 1988: 20; Stoneman et al., 1980: 433; Sobol and Cardiff, 1983: 483; Simpson et al., 1981: 433). For all but one of the adoptees in this study, the decision to make contact came quickly. One contacted the birth mother within a two-week period after learning her identity. Forty-four (73 per cent) contacted her within the first twenty-four hours. The investment of self demanded by the search had increased their desire for a meeting. As one adoptee claimed, 'I needed face-to-face contact. I don't know why. Probably because you envision something and you would like to see an end product. Not seeing her and getting all of your information would be like doing a project and not getting your final grade. You've put all of that time and effort into it. Also, there are questions that only she can answer. You need face-to-face contact to be able to ask them' (female, age 38).

Despite the short period between identification of the birth mother and contact with her, these adoptees experienced considerable anxiety over their decision to make contact. Contact with the birth mother connects adoptees to an unknown woman who possesses a separate identity and lives within a separate social world. These adoptees were uncertain, therefore, about the birth mother's reaction to contact. Yet because adoptees' increasing involvement in the search process compelled them to make contact, this anxiety emerged more in their decision over *how* rather than whether contact should be made. Thus, for example, those adoptees who found negative background information reported, 'I still had to see her. I tried to protect myself. The background information wasn't that good so I decided not to give her my last name or address in case she tried to get too involved. But I still had to see her. Face-to-face. I had to find out who I looked like and where I came from. I had come too far to back out now' (male, age 24). These types of precautionary measures indicate these adoptees' awareness of the birth mother as an active participant in the outcome of the reunion. The attempt to protect self from a possible negative experience in their contact with the birth mother demonstrates their internalization of the normative values supporting non-disclosure.

MOTIVE TALK, NON-DISCLOSURE, AND THE USE OF CONTACT INTERMEDIARIES

Understanding the dynamics of adoptee–birth mother contact requires an understanding of motive talk. One of the most significant rewards produced by human interaction is the social approval of others. A principal way to gain that social approval is through the proper use of motives. We use motives to describe our relationship to others, our social position, our past, present, and future behaviour. We tend, also, to explain other people's behaviour in those terms. We question others about their motives, impute motives to their unexplained behaviour, and respond to requests to explain others' motivations. In this way, motives become an attempt by us to summarize and make some sense out of the complex acts that compose our daily lives.

These motives take the form of 'vocabularies' that can be drawn upon to justify or explain action (Mills, 1940: 904). Because we gain a positive assessment of self through the reflected appraisals of others, our motive talk corresponds with society's normative values and social expectations. Those normative values give us a sense of which motives provide acceptable accounts of social behaviour and which do not. They help us assess the level of acceptability in our own motive talk and evaluate the motive talk employed by others. In this way an examination of motive talk provides a fairly concise picture of a society's rules, the members' assimilation of those rules, and an individual's position relative to others in that society.

The institution of adoption provides a vocabulary of motives that explains the protections offered by non-disclosure for each member of the adoption triangle. As members of their society, and, as specific members of the adoption triangle, adoptees know this vocabulary. Thus, for example, Sachdev (1992: 61) found that 'the adoptees' two most gripping fears before the meeting were that their search could be construed as being disloyal to the adoptive parents and that it could prove disruptive to the biological mother's life. They were also afraid that the biological mother might not be interested in them and they would face a second rejection.'

These fears resemble the three main motives for non-disclosure in adoption. Non-disclosure was enacted (1) to ensure the primacy of the adoptive parent–child relationship, (2) to protect the birth mother's confidentiality, and (3) to shelter the adoptee from contact with disreputable and irresponsible birth parents (Benet, 1976: 15; Garber, 1985; Griffith, 1991). When searching adoptees express the types of fear found by Sachdev, they demonstrate their own internalization of the normative values supporting non-disclosure. In this way, the vocabulary of motives used to support non-disclosure affects adoptees' perception of their adoptive status, their view of the position held by other members in the adoption triad, their postponement and ultimate decision to search, their contact with the birth mother, and the dynamics of their adoptee–birth mother interactions.

The accounts used by these adoptees in Chapter 3 to explain their postponement of search exemplify how adoptees internalize the motive talk used to support the adoptive parents' need for non-disclosure. This motive talk was apparent also when these adoptees discussed their decision about asking their adoptive parents for their adoption order. It arose, once again, when they discussed the decision-making process involved in contact with the birth mother.

Of the three members in the adoption triangle, adoptive parents are the most threatened by contact with the birth mother (Depp, 1982; Gonyo and Watson, 1988; Sorosky et al., 1978; Stoneman et al., 1980). Searching adoptees perceive their adoptive parents' fear of contact with the birth mother as a fear over the potential loss of their children to the birth parents (Gonyo and Watson, 1988: 19; Pacheco and Eme, 1993: 57; Sachdev, 1992: 60). In recognition of this fear, the adoptees in this study used various management techniques to cope with their anxiety over their adoptive parents' reactions to their search. Those management techniques matched their adoptive parents' own method of dealing with the topic of contact with the birth mother when it arose in their adoptive parent-child interactions. The relative success of those management techniques led these adoptees to use similar methods to handle their adoptive parents' reaction to their decision to contact the birth mother. Thus, 'avoidant' adoptees kept their contact attempt secret from their parents, 'open' adoptees discussed it with them, and 'pretence' adoptees never mentioned the event after they learned their birth name. In this way, these adoptees protected self and their adoptive parent–child relationship from the threat of contact with the birth mother. Yet rather than explaining those management techniques as a protection of self, these adoptees explained them in terms of their adoptive parents' position in the adoption triad, and their adoptive parents' need for non-disclosure.

The development of management techniques to handle the adoptees' anxiety over contact with the birth mother was more complex. These adoptees were sensitive to the birth mother's position as an active participant in the outcome of the reunion process. That sensitivity was influenced by their perception of non-disclosure as a protection of the birth mother's confidentiality. They worried, therefore, about the possible effects of contact on the birth mother's privacy. One adoptee reported that 'you have to be careful about contact. Back in those days, at least until up to twenty years ago, birth mothers were guaranteed complete confidentiality. They thought that they would never be found. That the adoption of a child was like the death of a child and they would never see that child again. It would be a great shock to her. Contact has to be made as carefully as possible. You don't want to upset her any more than you have to' (male, age 42). In this way, the motive talk used by their society to justify the birth mother's need for non-disclosure influenced the adoptees' decision over how to initiate contact.

The majority of these adoptees (forty-nine or 82 per cent) gave this concern for the birth mother's reaction to her loss of confidentiality as the reason for their use of intermediary contact devices. Those intermediary devices included personal letters, the Adoption Disclosure Register, birth relatives, and Parent Finders members (see Table 5.1). These adoptees explained their use of an intermediate contact device as a protection for the

TABLE 5.1
Method of contact and response of birth mother (rounded to nearest per cent) (N = 60)

Type of contact	Rejection		Acceptance		Cautious		Total	
	N	%	N	%	N	%	N	%
Phone call	3	20	5	19	3	21	11	18
Letter	1	7	2	8	0	0	3	5
Birth relative	4	27	2	8	4	29	10	17
Newspaper	1	7	0	0	0	0	1	2
Registry	0	0	2	8	0	0	2	3
Parent Finders	6	40	15	58	7	50	28	47
Deceased	–	–	–	–	–	–	5	8
Total	15	101	26	101	14	100	60	100

birth mother who could accustom herself to her loss of privacy and get over the shock of being found. To quote a frequent Parent Finders intermediary,

It is important to have someone who has experience in talking people down. A lot of birth mothers ask what the adoptee wants of them. That's very common. I am very honest about everything I say. I believe that comes across. Where the adoptee may often begin with one statement and then cross it with another. Because he's emotionally upset. I know the different kinds of questions that birth mothers ask and the different things that it helps them to hear. You can't minimize the fact that the kind of experience that you have in this area helps. I have made a lot of successful contacts and helped birth mothers come to terms with reunion when they express doubts about what they should do. (Female, age 42)

For this reason only eleven (18 per cent) of the interviewed adoptees telephoned the birth mother personally. These 'self-contact' adoptees had been too excited by their discovery of the birth mother's identity to wait for an intermediary to approach her on their behalf. They viewed contact also as a part of their search and reunion experience. If the birth mother rejected their contact, they wanted the opportunity to speak with her and try to get their questions answered 'before she hung up.' If she accepted contact, they wanted to experience her initial excitement of being found. Thus, a member of this group replied, 'I decided to call her myself. I wasn't sure if I'd ever get another chance to talk to her again. I wanted to get it all out because I thought that it might be the last chance for me. I was going to take that chance. At least, no matter what she said, I would have that conversation' (female, age 34).

Ten (17 per cent) of the adoptees used birth relatives to contact the birth mother. These birth relative contacts had been established through 'fishing' calls during the search. When the birth relative became suspicious about the personal tone of the questions being asked, these adoptees had revealed their true identity. Upon learning that identity, the birth relative offered to act as an intermediary and approach the birth mother for a meeting.

These 'fishing call' situations stress the need for more direct reunion assistance by legislative and social service bodies involved in adoption (Garber, 1985: 47; Sachdev, 1989). Despite this sample's apparent commitment to the birth mother's confidentiality, their search tactics exposed her status as the birth mother to others without her consent. Six of these ten birth relative intermediaries had no knowledge of the birth mother's relinquishment before the adoptee's call. In addition, two adoptees in this study met the birth mother accidentally when they knocked on her door looking for a birth relative who might provide further background material. Both of these birth mothers were hostile when they learned the adoptee's identity. Although both birth mothers established contact with the adoptee at a later date, this first meeting tainted future birth mother–adoptee interactions.

Twenty-six (43 per cent) used Parent Finders intermediaries. This group of adoptees viewed Parent Finders as a professional agency with considerable experience in contact situations. They believed a Parent Finders intermediary would ease the shock of contact and give the birth mother an opportunity to discuss her situation with a sympathetic other who had prior experience of this type of contact. The adoptees' own feelings of acceptance at Parent Finders meetings substantiated their trust in that intermediary to promote their search concerns and effect satisfactory contact. As one Parent Finders intermediary explained, 'Using someone else gives her time to adjust. The initial reaction is "Oh, My God! How is she? I couldn't possibly meet her." I think it's fear. Like, it took me forty-one years to search and it has taken my birth mother an equal amount of time to try to forget. My ideas of charging ahead and finding her must be compared to her trying to get it in the back of her mind as far as she can. An intermediary gives her time to get over the shock and think about it' (female, age 49).

The use of contact intermediaries is common for searching adoptees (Gonyo and Watson, 1988). For example, 65 per cent of Sachdev's sample (1992) used a third party to establish birth mother contact. Like the adoptees in this study, Sachdev's adoptees (1992: 61) 'described the intermediary as helpful in resolving the anxiety, uncertainty, and compunction' experienced over contact with the birth mother. Also, the majority of Sachdev's sample used Parent Finders intermediaries. Although Parent Finders offers non-professional contact, these adoptees believed that the intermediary's own search and reunion experience gave him or her a better sensitivity to the birth mother's reaction and a stronger understanding of the issues involved in contact with the birth mother.

Yet, despite this concern over method of contact, no significant relationship existed between the method of contact used and the birth mother's acceptance or rejection of contact. Table 5.1 shows the same range of reactions of the birth mother for self-contact adoptees as those given to adoptees who used intermediary devices. In addition, Sachdev (1992: 63) notes that 'the initial reactions of the biological mother were not an indicator of how the relationship might continue.' For example, of the eleven 'self-contact' approaches in this study, five birth mothers accepted the adoptee immediately, three were initially suspicious but accepted contact later, and three denied any knowledge of the adoptee's existence. The birth mother's own perception of, and desire for, contact is a more significant factor in the outcome of contact than the method of contact used (Gonyo and Watson, 1988; Pacheco and Eme, 1993; Sachdev, 1992).

The adoptees in this study accepted the birth mother's decision about contact with little protest. Of particular note was the acceptance by adoptees who used third-party intermediaries. These adoptees did not question the intermediary's description of the birth mother's response. None of them tried a later contact of their own. In fact, the intermediary's definition of the situation became their own definition of the outcome of contact. One replied, 'The woman who called from Parent Finders told me that she was very nice and polite. She didn't deny it. She just said that she had her own life. I had mine. It was best to leave it like that. I never bothered her again. Her husband doesn't know. It hurts because you don't think that you will be rejected. I respect her position. I never tried to contact her again. I never even went to try to see her, even though I know where she lives and where she works. I don't want to intrude. It's over. She decided. I respect her decision' (female, age 40). Another stated, 'The lady from Parent Finders called and explained the situation to her. She didn't agree to everything right away. I guess, she wanted to think it over. It was a sudden shock after twenty-one years to know that all of a sudden your son is calling you. By the end of the call, she agreed. Then, the lady from Parent Finders called me and told me that she would be calling me in five minutes. That was the start of it' (male, age 24). Still another explained, 'I wouldn't make the call myself. You're so up. You really don't know what you are saying. They are good at it. So, I asked Parent Finders to make the call. They called while I was at work. The woman called me and said, "I've just spoken to the happiest woman in the world." I burst into tears right in the middle of the office. It was really quite emotional. She was really happy. She kept saying to them, "You've found my baby." I phoned her that night and we made arrangements to meet' (female, age 42).

These quotes demonstrate how the use of third-party contact protects self as well as the birth mother. The majority of these adoptees knew the birth mother's name, address, and many personal facts about her past and present life before they initiated contact. A large number had jeopardized her confidentiality several times during the search process. Intermediaries were used, therefore, for other reasons than birth mother confidentiality. They were used also to protect the adoptee from the impact of a second rejection. These adoptees were aware of their vulnerable position as biological children requesting contact with a woman who had symbolically rejected them through the act of relinquishment. Intermediaries could soften the blow of a possible second rejection by censoring their account of the birth mother's initial reaction to contact and any negative statements produced by her shock at being identified. For this reason, the young man above could accept 'she didn't agree to everything right away.' He did not have a haunting memory of the exact wording used by his birth mother. He did not encounter any personal sense of rejection by her as she tried to sort through the thoughts and emotions arising during that first contact call.

RELINQUISHMENT, PERCEPTION OF THE POWER OF THE BIRTH MOTHER, AND FEAR OF A SECOND REJECTION

In the same way as rejection represented a latent concern in these adoptees' discussion of their initial contact with the birth mother, it served as an underlying theme in the assessment of continued contact. For example, in their explanation of postponement of the search in Chapter 3, only six (5 per cent) of the 113 responses given by the adoptees in this study referred to 'fear of rejection' as a cause for delay (see Tables 3.3 and 3.4). In addition, although thirty-five (58 per cent) of these adoptees defined unsuccessful contact with the birth mother as 'rejection,' only nine (15 per cent) had considered rejection as a possible result of contact with their own birth mother. The majority claimed something similar to the following adoptee who said, 'I wasn't really afraid of rejection. I kind of figured that her curiosity

would get to her too. That she would be the same as me in that way. For-
tunately for me she was glad that I found her. Because, I think that all
adoptees feel rejected from day one. Like, mothers just don't give their kids
away' (female, age 29).

These adoptees had internalized the negative stereotypes carried by birth
mothers in our society. They were aware also of their stigmatized status
as 'rejected' birth children. If they had considered rejection as a possible
result of the search, they may not have made the total investment of self
that the search demanded. They had perceived rejection, therefore, as a possibility only for other adoptees. When they initiated contact with the birth
mother, they could no longer ignore the possibility of their own rejection.
They, therefore, used third-party contact to insulate themselves from that
possible second rejection. As one woman observed, 'I should have considered
rejection but I didn't. I had a lot to lose. If she had said that she didn't
want to see me, I would have been devastated. I guess, I thought that I
was worth knowing. I thought that I would be someone special to her. If
she didn't want to accept me, then, I think that I would have been destroyed.
I had this thing in my head that, "Of course, she would want to see me.
How could she not want me?" I was a real gambler because I would have
been emotionally upset if she had rejected me again' (female, age 36).

Our society promotes a 'motherhood myth' in which all women desire
children who they will nurture into adulthood (Caplan, 1989; Chodorow,
1978; Levine and Estable, 1990). The act of relinquishment contradicts this
image of 'mother' as tender, affectionate, constantly present and self-
sacrificing. Women who relinquish their children are punished for their de-
viance and labelled as unfeeling and self-centred (Inglis, 1984). Their relinquished children are perceived as unworthy products discarded by uncaring
mothers (Benet, 1976: 14). To counteract this message, adoptees receive a
'chosen child' story in which their adoptive parents select them specifically
to become a member of their family (Garber, 1985: 12). Yet this chosen
child story does not eliminate the underlying message of rejection signified
by a birth mother who renounces her maternity. One of the adoptees in
this study, therefore remarked that, 'all that stuff about the chosen child
only hides the truth. That someone out there didn't choose you. In order
to cover that, they form this romantic ideal of a young mother that had
to give you up and suffers in silence and still wants you. That is the story
that you are told. And that you want to believe. But everybody believes
differently. They all believe that you weren't wanted. So, to search, you are
taking a big risk. Because, if you find out differently, it's really disappointing.
Because, then, you really know that you were unchosen' (female, age 43).

Another said, 'that she was nice to me and seemed to care what happened was important. That meant a lot to me. Even at the Children's Aid Society, they said she was a caring person. She wasn't some toughie in prison that had babies every year out of wedlock. I remember that. I remember feeling excited when I left their office. Just knowing, "Gee, she cared about me." That made me feel really good. That she cared what happened to me' (female, age 37).

In this way, these adoptees' recognition of their social status as children who are 'unchosen' and, then, 'chosen' influenced the dynamics of contact with the birth mother. Their symbolic rejection through the birth mother's original relinquishment created anxiety over her present acceptance of them. When they combined that fear with their uncertainty over their intrusion into the birth mother's life, they experienced a sense of powerlessness with regard to the outcome of contact. Thus, one of the adoptees in this study claimed that 'once you have made the initial contact, you have to follow her way. Otherwise, you are intruding. She's the one that holds the key to everything that you want to know. And, she'll let you know exactly what she wants you to know and no more. She is in a power position. That's why she has to be given time and space after you contact her. You have to let her make a lot of the decisions about the reunion and how it is to proceed. Because you are the one intruding into her life' (female, age 49). This perception of the birth mother's position of power to determine contact contributed greatly to the types of adoptee–birth mother interactions described in the following sections.

TYPES OF CONTACT WITH THE BIRTH MOTHER

Media stories, Parent Finders presentations, and the early reunion research literature concentrate on 'acceptance' or 'rejection' as the two major types of contact outcome (Sorosky et al., 1978; Stoneman et al., 1980; Thompson et al., 1978; Triseliotis, 1973). Recently a more complex picture of contact with the birth mother has emerged. Pacheco and Eme (1993: 6) found that the frequency of contact with the birth mother tends to 'take the pattern of a period of great intensity followed by diminished frequency, with the most common pattern being monthly/bimonthly or holidays (45 per cent).' Sachdev (1992: 63) reported also that over half of his sample saw each other regularly, while one-fifth saw each other occasionally and 17 per cent terminated their relationships after the first meeting. In both studies, the majority of the adoptees described their contact relationship as 'friendship.' These findings suggest a continuum of contact types ranging from immediate rejection to deep intimacy.

In this study, contact with the birth mother falls within three main types: (1) discontinuation of contact by the birth mother, (2) discontinuation of contact by the adoptee, and (3) continued contact. Discontinuation of contact by the birth mother includes immediate rejection, gradual disengagement, and death. Some adoptees discontinued contact when they found a birth mother who disrupted their life. This outcome of contact represents a different adoptee–birth mother interaction pattern than the others. The majority maintained some form of continued contact. Although many birth mothers limited contact because other members of their family do not know of their relinquishment, most of the birth mothers welcomed the adoptee openly into their family structure. In this way 'acceptance' and 'rejection' represent the end categories of a continuum of contact that reflected the needs of both birth mother and adoptee.

DISCONTINUATION OF CONTACT BY THE BIRTH MOTHER

Immediate Rejection

Eight (13 per cent) of the adoptees in this study experienced immediate rejection by the birth mother (see Table 5.2). These adoptees decided not to make a second attempt at contact because, as one of them said, 'It was better to stay away. Just to let it lie. She's been through a lot. I think that the experience of having me had a devastating effect on her. After her attitude and her reaction when she was contacted, there's nothing more really. I've got the information that I really needed. She's got her life and I've got mine. We should leave it like that' (female, age 30). Another maintained, 'There's no sense pushing it. I don't think that she could accept it because she is from a different generation. She denied it so long. Her husband and children don't know. It was too hard for her to accept, I guess' (female, age 40).

Rather than viewing the birth mother's denial of contact as a personal rejection, these adoptees explained it as a combination of the traumatic events surrounding their conception, birth, and relinquishment and the birth mother's fear of the loss of confidentiality promised by non-disclosure. This belief made the birth mother's rejection of contact less personal. It also protected the adoptee's image of self as a 'child' who was valued by her. By not seeking an account of her actions and withdrawing from further contact, they ensured the effectiveness of these imputed motives. Thus, despite their 'disappointment,' 'frustration,' and 'remorse' over the birth mother's response to contact, one of these adoptees could state, 'I didn't see it as a rejection, really. I felt sorry for this old lady. Imagine this happening

TABLE 5.2
Type of contact established by adoptees with birth mother (rounded to nearest per cent)
(N = 60)

Birth mother contact	Males		Females		Total	
	N	%	N	%	N	%
Rejection	1	6	7	16	8	13
Disengaged	3	19	6	14	9	15
Rejection of birth mother	2	13	5	11	7	12
Limited contact	1	6	6	14	7	12
Open contact	8	50	16	36	24	40
Birth mother deceased	1	6	4	9	5	8
Total	16	100	44	100	60	100

to her at that time of her life. I've lived without this for such a long time that it's not going to make me or break me. My own mother was so good. You don't need anybody else after her. I really didn't need to meet this lady. I just wanted some information for my children and my grandchildren' (female, age 65).

These adoptees also discounted the impact of rejection by referring to their adoptive identity and the primacy of their adoptive parent–child relationship. Like the adoptee above, they rationalized their sense of rejection through their explanation of the search as a desire for genealogical information. Continued contact with the birth mother had been an additional bonus. In this way, they transformed the vocabulary of motives used to support non-disclosure to fit their contact results. They protected themselves from the full impact of a second rejection by the birth mother by viewing the birth mother's response as a rejection of her status as a birth mother rather than as a denial of them personally.

Gradual Disengagement

Nine (15 per cent) of the interviewed adoptees in this study experienced gradual disengagement from contact. Three never met with the birth mother but exchanged several letters and telephone calls with her before she discontinued contact. The remaining six met with the birth mother at least once. None of these 'disengaged' adoptees asked the birth mother for an account of her behaviour. Like the 'rejected' adoptees, they applied their own motives to her actions. They referred to her stigmatized position in the adoption triangle, the difficulties involved in open contact, and the painful memories of a traumatic relinquishment. In this way, these adoptees explained the birth mother's withdrawal from contact as a rejection of the social stigma carried by birth mothers rather than as a rejection of themselves. As one of them replied, 'I think that she cut off contact because she was afraid that other people would find out who I was. She hadn't told her family. She was scared. I can understand that. She lives in a small community and she's lived there all her life. People might start asking who is this strange person coming to visit all the time. I know that if I need any more information that I can call her. Really that's all I need. I have my parents. They are my family. Not her. She can just tell me some things about myself that they can't' (female, age 29).

Like the previous group, these 'disengaged' adoptees used the primacy of their adoptive parent–child bonds to support their sense of value as a child who was 'wanted' by others. They did, however, express more distress over their contact outcome, because they could not be certain whether their definition of the situation was accurate. The birth mother's initial acceptance and subsequent disengagement left them wondering whether she had rejected *them* rather than the idea of contact. One adoptee noted that 'she accepted me, but she didn't. Which isn't as bad as an outright rejection, I guess. But it isn't the same thing as an outright acceptance either. She really didn't take the time to be with me and get to know me. Although the fact that she was excited was good for me. It's just that she couldn't accept me outside. Like, others knowing about me. I am still confused over her behaviour. I guess that's how she wants it so I have decided to just let it be' (female, age 39). Another said, 'I don't see it as a rejection. I am disappointed. I sometimes think about phoning her but I haven't done it. I guess she wants it that way. She knows our address and she knows where I live as well as I know where she is. She did break off contact. I'm not going to push myself on her. I can re-establish contact if I want. The time just isn't right. I guess that I'm stubborn too' (female, age 29).

Yet by refusing to ask the birth mother for an explanation of her disengagement, these adoptees protected themselves from a possible second rejection from her and safeguarded their perception of self as a child who had not been 'unchosen.' They reinforced that perception by referring to the risks taken by the birth mother when she arranged their contact meeting and her availability for future contact if they desired. Several mentioned, also, that their search was motivated by a need for genealogical and genetic information rather than contact with the birth mother. In this way, contact with the birth mother became an additional but, unexpected, bonus of the search. As one man put it, 'It was an experience. If you had got me two years ago when it happened, I would have been more excited. Now, I have other concerns. My curiosity was satisfied. That was all I wanted. That was enough. Meeting her was nice because I got to know who I looked like and who she was. Things like that. It was enough. I didn't want any more' (male, age 30).

Birth Mother Deceased

Five (8 per cent) adoptees found the birth mother deceased. Like the adoptees who experienced rejection, these adoptees had not prepared themselves fully for this possible outcome of search. If they had, they might not have made the total investment of self demanded by the search. The outcome of this type of contact resembled the stages of grief encountered by people who experience a significant loss (Kubler-Ross, 1970). These stages are (1) denial and isolation, (2) anger, (3) bargaining, (4) depression, and (5) acceptance. At first, the adoptees who discovered the birth mother deceased were shocked and denied their search findings by investigating further into the circumstances involved in the birth mother's death. Thus, three of these adoptees searched for and visited the birth mother's grave 'just so I could see and believe that she was a real person and that she was dead.' Another obtained copies of the birth mother's death certificate and autopsy report. One went to the birth mother's former neighbourhood and questioned people about her life. These symbolic contact gestures established the existence of a 'real' person who represented the adoptees' biological connection to others. As such, these actions established the adoptees' search objectives and validated the investment of self required by their search.

Verification of the birth mother's death made these adoptees angry at themselves for their postponement of their search. They lessened that anger during a bargaining stage in which they decided to contact other birth relatives for more genealogical and genetic information. Acceptance by these other birth relatives and receipt of additional background information helped these adoptees reconcile themselves to their search findings and the inevitability of the birth mother's death.

This group was distressed by their missed opportunity to engage in contact with the birth mother. Although contact with other birth relatives provided these adoptees with a biological connection and a birth family history, they felt 'cheated' and 'deprived' of the chance to communicate directly with a birth mother who might have offered some feeling of attachment to them. Like the 'disengaged' adoptees, they could not experience closure of the search. This group expressed the greatest disappointment, therefore, with the outcome of their search and more anger at the demand for non-disclosure than any of the other adoptees in this study. The following quote describes the grief process involved in this outcome of search:

I was in the library when I found out that she was dead. I was shocked. She was missing from the directory. I wasn't positive but it was my clue. I went from there to find the death certificate. I was excited before I found out that she was dead because I knew that she was actually a person who had an address that I could track down. When I found out that she was dead, I was angry. I had come this far only to find her dead.

After a time, I wrote to her husband. He did not know about me. He was very friendly and told me a lot of things about her that I didn't know. It helped because it filled in some of the gaps. It made me extremely resentful too because I didn't get to know her.

Now, I'm sad. I'm sad that I missed the opportunity. I'm still at loose ends. I regret that I didn't take the risk sooner. Like, stop worrying about the negative and think about the positive. Take the risk because tomorrow might not come. They may die in the meantime.

I still get down sometimes when I think about it. It's not fair that the people who brought us into the world are hidden to us. That everyone else can find out or already know but we can't. It's not a long depression. But I still think it's unfair that I never got to know her' (female, age 55).

DISCONTINUATION OF CONTACT BY THE ADOPTEE

Rejection of Contact with the Birth Mother

Seven (12 per cent) adoptees rejected contact with their birth mother. Three members of this group decided not to contact the birth mother at all. These three adoptees had found information that revealed the birth mother as 'the welfare type,' 'an alcoholic,' and 'sexually promiscuous.' When birth relatives confirmed their search findings these adoptees abandoned the idea of a meeting with the birth mother. Thus, one explained her rejection of contact with her birth mother as

a logical choice. I got very negative background information from the Children's Aid. I contacted my birth grandmother and she told me the same things. So, I decided not to contact my birth mother. I really didn't want a relationship. I just wanted background information. I keep contact with my birth grandmother. I consider this woman a friend but she thinks of me as her granddaughter. But she has not replaced anybody. My own parents are still in my life. It was just a nice feeling to meet her because she bothered to take the time to show up. It showed that she cared for me. To know who you look like, medical information, and things in your background. It filled in all the blanks for me. I didn't have to meet my birth mother for that' (female, age 42)

Although the remaining four adoptees received similar descriptions of their birth mother, their obsession with search stimulated their desire for contact with her. However, when they found the birth mother's behaviour too erratic and difficult for them to handle, they also severed contact. As one of these adoptees explained, 'I figured everybody has problems. The things I learned about her didn't bother me. It was more her attitude toward life. She had five of us. One after the other. She gave us all up for adoption. She didn't feel bad about it. Her attitude was "Easy come, easy go." Not that I wanted her stricken with guilt for the rest of her days but she acted like we didn't mean very much. Then, I kept getting the runaround. She wouldn't answer my questions and the ones she did answer, I didn't know if I could believe them. There was no reason to continue' (female, age 24).

These adoptees took greater risks with self than did the other three. They drew limits on those risks when they found 'rejecting' birth mothers. Although the birth mother accepted contact, her actions revealed little concern for the adoptee's needs and little interest in the adoptee as a person. These adoptees withdrew from contact when they perceived such contact held no value for the birth mother. More than any other group these adoptees needed an explanation for their birth mother's attitude that would protect their perception of self as valued. To achieve this goal, they turned to their adoptive parents and the chosen child message that had been offered them to support non-disclosure. These explanations helped them distance themselves from their birth mother's behaviour and disconnect from problematic contact with an undesirable birth mother.

CONTINUED CONTACT

Conditional Acceptance and Limited Contact

Seven (12 per cent) of these adoptees found a birth mother who had not told her spouse or subsequent children about her earlier relinquishment of a child. These birth mothers arranged secret meetings with the adoptee that ranged from two hours at a restaurant or friend's home to two days in a motel room. During those contact meetings, the birth mother answered the adoptees' questions openly and provided as much background information as she could. For this reason, these adoptees perceived the birth mother's conditional contact as a reaction to her current life situation rather than as a rejection of them personally. They viewed her arrangement of secret contact as a symbolic gesture that signified her motherly concern for them. These 'conditional contact' adoptees experienced an incredible sense of responsibility, therefore, to maintain the birth mother's confidentiality. In this way, conditional contact bonded birth parent and adoptee together in a new alliance of secrecy and trust. To quote one 'conditional contact' adoptee,

I think that she was glad that I found her. We have a mutual understanding between us and there is a trust bond between us because she has other children and they don't know. Nobody knows. It is a painful thing to her. There is a tremendous amount of guilt. She said that going through that experience at that time you didn't get any sympathy from anybody. They were told that they would never see their baby again. I know there was a lot of caring. When you are doing something like this you always have to respect the other person. We're all human and some of us are more scared than others. I accept that she can't acknowledge me openly' (female, age 36)

Three of these adoptees developed a friendship with the birth mother. They went shopping, met for lunch, and telephoned back and forth. One woman became a volunteer driver for a birth family member who needed regular medical treatments but who did not know her full identity. Although these adoptees desired a more open acknowledgment of their birth status by their birth mothers, they accepted this pretence relationship. The secrecy inherent in adoption had prepared them for these covert roles. One of them observed that 'it's not the best situation. But we both know about each other's lives. Knowing her and just being able to get my questions answered and being able to see each other and keep up to date. That's enough. She has a lot to lose if people find out. I was lucky that she wanted to meet me and wasn't afraid to. A lot of them are so afraid that meeting you is going to totally disrupt their lives that they refuse to do it. She trusted me and I agreed. I'm satisfied' (female, age 35).

These 'conditional contact' adoptees used the birth mother's stigmatized status, her expectation of life-long confidentiality, and her precarious family position to explain the outcome of contact. They viewed the birth mother's trust in their ability to keep her confidentiality as part of the bargain made during their first attempt at contact. As such, this type of contact with the birth mother increased these adoptees' perception of self as a person who was valued by her. The birth mother's willingness to risk exposure of her status as a birth mother through face-to-face contact fit the definition of a caring mother who made sacrifices for her child.

Open Contact

Twenty-four (40 per cent) adoptees achieved unrestricted contact with their birth mother. In all of these cases, the birth mother acknowledged the adoptee publicly as her relinquished child. Nine birth mothers had kept their relinquishment a secret from their other children. However, unlike the 'conditional contact' birth mothers, the husbands of these 'open' birth mothers had known about the adoptee before contact. This finding signifies the husband–wife relationship as a more significant variable in contact than the parent–child relationship. Stoneman et al. (1980: 19) and Sachdev (1992: 63) report, for instance, that conflict in the birth mother–adoptee relationship occurs when a birth mother's husband becomes unwilling to accept the adoptee. Although the 'open contact' adoptees in this study made no mention of such conflict, the experience of 'conditional contact' adoptees indicates the need for more study on the impact of both adoptive and birth family members on contact with the birth mother.

The 'open contact' birth mothers welcomed the adoptee as a full member of the birth family. They readily discussed the adoptee's genetic and genealogical background, revealed the birth father's identity, and talked about the events surrounding the adoptee's conception, birth, and relinquishment. These adoptees perceived this openness as a reflection of the birth mother's interest in them and her continued concern for their personal welfare despite her relinquishment. However, because her behaviour contradicted their expectation of rejection, one of them described the outcome of contact as 'a surprise. I didn't expect any relationship. That was icing on the cake. That she was nice to me. That she seemed to care what had happened to me. That meant a lot to me. When she asked to see me again, I said, "Okay." It meant something to her. It was nice to know that. That's how it all started' (female, age 36).

The normative constraints held against contact with the birth mother produce uncertainty over the adoptee–birth parent relationship. No rules of interaction have been established for this type of social situation, and no guidelines have been formulated for the social obligations existing between birth mother and adoptee. Both actors enter an ambiguous process of negotiation of roles as they outline the parameters of contact with the birth mother. The adoptees in this study used the vocabulary of motives linked to non-disclosure to explain that process of contact. By offering them an acceptable account of each person's position in the adoption triangle that vocabulary of motives helped these adoptees make sense of the complex acts involved in contact with their birth mother.

Like other searchers (Gonyo and Watson, 1988; Pacheco and Eme, 1993; Sachdev, 1992), these adoptees expressed concern about their adoptive parents' reaction to their desire for contact with the birth mother. Many had postponed the search to avoid any feeling of hurt or betrayal by their adoptive parents. Others used pretence awareness contexts to counteract their adoptive parents' anxiety about the search for or contact with the birth mother. In this way, we can see how the adoptees' knowledge of their adoptive parents' position in the adoption triangle affected their decision to exclude their adoptive parents from the search process and influenced their desire to protect their adoptive parent–child relationship from any possible damage caused by contact with their birth mother.

In a similar fashion, adoptees understand the use of non-disclosure as a protection for the position of the birth mother. The adoptees in this study expressed that understanding through their use of an intermediary contact who was sensitive to the birth mother's need for confidentiality and responsive to her possible shock from their initial contact. Like other searchers (Gonyo and Watson, 1988; Pacheco and Eme, 1993; Sachdev, 1992), these adoptees explained their use of third-party contact as a concern that the birth mother might be agitated or disturbed by the adoptees' direct contact. In addition, they claimed uncertainty over her current family situation and did not want to intrude into her life.

The adoptees' awareness of their own adoptive status contributed greatly, however, to the decision regarding contact. Non-disclosure safeguards adoptees from open confrontation with the questionable moral background of birth parents who have conceived them under suspicious circumstances (Benet, 1976: 15; Garber, 1985: 13). In addition, the motherhood myth and the underlying message of rejection in the 'chosen child' story presuppose a possible second rejection upon contact with the birth mother. The decision to use an intermediary protected these adoptees from the full impact of this possible second rejection.

The underlying message of rejection through adoption holds particular significance for the examination of the outcome of contact. Adoptees put aside the possibility of a personal rejection when they engage in the process of search. During their decision to make contact, they begin to anticipate – and prepare for – a second rejection. This expectation of a second rejection inhibits their ability to ask the birth mother for an explanation of her response to contact or of her behaviour towards them. Instead, they take the vocabulary of motives used to justify non-disclosure and apply it to their experience of contact. Like the motive talk accompanying non-disclosure, this motive talk focuses on three major themes. They are (1) rejection of the adoptee by an uncaring birth mother, (2) disruption of the birth mother's privacy, and (3) the primacy of the adoptive parent–child relationship. Thus, 'rejected' adoptees explained their rejection as a reaction by the birth mother to the trauma of her relinquishment, 'disengaged' adoptees disclaimed a sense of rejection by referring to their strong adoptive parent–child bonds, and 'limited contact' adoptees justified their pretence contact relationships as a protection of the birth mother's current life situation.

Adoptees who experience 'open' contact with their birth mothers face a different dilemma. When adoptees make the decision to contact the birth mother, they prepare for rejection. What they are not prepared for is acceptance. Once acceptance occurs, adoptees must find a way 'to bridge the gap of time and experience and to establish a meaningful tie to the "stranger" who is so much a part' of them (Gonyo and Watson, 1988: 20). In addition, few birth mothers are prepared for contact with the adoptee (Silverman et al., 1988; Stoneman et al., 1980). However, those birth mothers who accept contact become active participants in the reunion process with a reunion agenda of their own. Contact becomes a process of negotiation of roles in which both the birth mother and the adoptee mediate their needs for contact and the type of contact relationship to be maintained. The next chapter examines the dynamics of this role-negotiation process for the adoptees who engage in long-term contact with their birth mothers.

6

Interaction of Adoptees and Birth Mothers, Negotiation of Roles, and Long-term Contact

Once the birth mother accepts contact, adoptees try to arrange a face-to-face meeting. During this stage of the contact, they discover a 'stranger' who demonstrates her own contact needs. This perception of meeting a 'stranger' rather than a 'mother' reinforces the adoptive identity established within the adoptive family structure. Adoptees who discover unfavourable background information or an undesirable contact with the birth mother use this adoptive identity to distance self from their reunion findings. Also, this sense of disconnection from the birth mother helps those adoptees in 'limited contact,' 'disengagement,' or 'rejecting' reunions to accept their outcome of contact more easily.

Few rules of conduct exist for the unconventional adoptee–birth mother relationship. Adoptees who engage in contact with the birth mother enter an uncertain process of negotiation of roles that is governed by their perception of the birth mother's affection for them. During that role-negotiation process, these adoptees turned to other role relationships for guidance in their adoptee–birth mother interactions. As a result, three main role relationships tended to develop: (1) duty, (2) friendship, and (3) parent–child. These role relationships reflect the balance drawn between the adoptees' recognition of the birth mother's own needs for contact and her acceptance of the adoptees' experience within the adoptive family structure.

THE FIRST MEETING

Face-to-face contact represents an important stage in the search and reunion process. At this time, adoptees validate their obscure genetic and genealogical information through a physical encounter with their primary biological connection (that is, the birth mother). Only thirty-eight (63 per cent) of the adoptees in this study achieved face-to-face contact with the birth mother. Table 6.1 outlines the adoptees' first impression of their birth mothers during their initial meeting. Like Pacheco and Eme's sample (1993: 60), many of these adoptees experienced a degree of disappointment in their birth mother. They were disappointed because the birth mother 'did not physically re-semble them,' 'was not like the adoptive family,' and appeared as a 'stranger.' One described her first meeting with her birth mother as 'very odd. When you tell people, they get all emotional and sentimental. That word "mother." It gives people a warm feeling. Because of what a mother means to you. Everybody thinks that you are experiencing that feeling. I certainly didn't. It was exciting to find her. But, it's not the same thing as though your mother had raised you and, then, all of a sudden, through circumstances of war, you lost her and you were reunited. It's not that sort of feeling at all. It's sort of empty. Because that could be anybody sitting there' (female, age 45). Another adoptee described the first meeting as 'strange. It was like walking in on anyone. I didn't have in mind, "This is my mother". When I saw her, I thought, "This is a stranger." There was no relationship. No feeling. In a way, she was just like any other person that I had to get to know' (female, age 41).

These adoptees had believed the motherhood myth that 'some magical bond exists between a biological mother and child which no amount of time or separation can eclipse' (Stoneman et al., 1980: 5). In accordance with this mythical expectation, they had envisioned an immediate attachment with the birth mother. Instead, they met a 'stranger.' The lack of mutual interaction in the years between relinquishment and contact had created a social gap that needed to be bridged if contact was to continue (Gonyo and Watson, 1988; Silverman et al., 1988). Like any two strangers who meet for the first time, both adoptee and birth mother had to negotiate their contact relationship. Some maintained contact until they found a way to bridge that gap. Others did not. For example, one woman replied, 'The thing that makes you close to your mother is not the fact that she bore you. It's the fact of all the things that she did for you all of your life. This person, although she is my biological mother, she doesn't remember any of that. So, I'm meeting another adult. Just the same as I'm meeting anyone. I met her on the basis of how she interacts with me. Like, mine is the kind of person that if I met her at the laudromat, I would be happy to know her. The fact that she's a blood relation and that she's happy that she got to know me makes me feel good. It's a bonus, really' (female, age 45). In this way, the first face-to-face meeting marks the beginning stage in a negotiation process between two individuals who must both desire,

TABLE 6.1
Adoptees' first impression of birth mother (rounded to nearest per cent) (N = 68)

Impression	First response		Second response		Total	
	N	%	N	%	N	%
Not like me	8	21	3	10	11	16
Nice, warm, open	12	32	9	30	21	30
Different from adoptive family	4	11	5	17	9	13
Lower class, loud, abrasive	7	18	3	10	10	15
Just like me	4	11	1	3	5	8
A 'stranger'	3	8	9	30	12	18
Total	38	101	30	100	68	100

and work at, the development of an acceptable adoptee–birth mother contact relationship. As a 'disengaged' man explained, 'This relationship is just like any other. It takes two to make it or break it. If you have a friend that you never see, and you give him a number of calls and he doesn't respond, you finally make a decision that maybe the relationship is more important to you than to that other person. You let it go. It was the same with her. Every time after our first meeting when I'd call to ask my birth mother to meet, she would say, "I'll let you know." She kept putting it off. I stopped calling. I really got tired of pushing myself on her. She was being rather difficult. That's how it ended up' (male, age 42).

The sensation of meeting a 'stranger' does not eliminate the strong emotions experienced during the first contact meeting (Gonyo and Watson, 1988: 20). These adoptees reported 'intense excitement,' 'euphoria,' and 'nervous tension' at the prospect of face-to-face contact with their birth mothers. After an initial period of numbness at the shock of her physical reality, both birth mother and adoptee cried, hugged, and scrutinized each for physical similarities. To ease the tension, they frequently engaged in neutral smalltalk, which led into more lengthy discussions of personal likes and dislikes, their present family situations, occupational interests, and so forth. Once a sense of mutual comfort was established, these adoptees raised their genetic and genealogical concerns and questioned the events surrounding their conception, birth, and relinquishment. The following quote describes a 'typical' first meeting:

Do you know what it is to run and run and feel like your heart is going to pop right out of your chest? That's how excited, I was. What it felt like to go there. Then, I walked in. I didn't know how to react. Should I run to her? Should I hug her? Do I kiss her? We ended up just looking at each other. After about five minutes or so, I think that we both walked over and hugged. We started to talk about my drive. Little things like that. After about an hour or so, we relaxed a bit. I started to ask her things about herself and she asked about me too. It was nerve-wracking. From the point of view that I didn't know what to expect or who to expect. What she was going to be like. It was very tense. (Female, age 26)

Like all social contacts, the other person's behaviour affects the inter-actional process. However, adoptees transfer the birth mother's power to determine the outcome of their initial contact to this second contact situation–the reunion. The birth mother's attitude determines the length and speed of transition from one stage to another. If, for example, she appears shy, withdrawn, or indifferent, then, adoptees are hesitant to ask for more genetic or genealogical information or to inquire about her relinquishment of them. If, she appears warm and accepting, then, adoptees may approach her more easily with their questions. Thus, in describing her own behaviour during her first face-to-face contact meeting, one woman said, 'I didn't want to be pushy. I felt lucky that she even wanted to see me. I figured that I was in no position to impose any kind of a relationship. We would play it by ear. If she wanted to call me once a week or every day, that would be fine. We would do it her way. I felt that I wasn't in any kind of a position to say anything. I felt privileged that she even wanted to meet me. So, when she didn't want to talk about things, I didn't push. I took what she told me and hoped that she would offer more. When she didn't, there was nothing else to do. I had to accept it' (female, age 26).

The majority of birth mothers understand the adoptees' need to contact them for more genetic and genealogical information (Anderson, 1989; Gonyo and Watson, 1988; Pacheco and Eme, 1993; Sachdev, 1992; Silverman et al., 1988). In addition, birth mothers' own 'lack of information about what happened to their baby and the strong feelings of attachment and separation they experienced' (Silverman et al., 1988: 525) through the relinquishment of their children motivate their own desire for contact as a way to resolve that past experience. These birth mothers responded positively, therefore, to the adoptees' request for more background information during this first face-to-face meeting. Of particular note were those women who risked exposure of their social status as birth mothers and met the adoptee secretly.

ATTITUDE OF THE BIRTH MOTHER, GESTURES OF CONCERN FOR THE ADOPTEE,
AND CONTINUED CONTACT

Of the thirty-eight adoptees who achieved a face-to-face meeting, only
twenty-four (40 per cent of the sample) developed an open contact relationship (see Table 6.2). These twenty-four adoptees found birth mothers
who openly requested continued contact. In addition, these birth mothers
made gestures that symbolized their continued concern for the adoptees
over the years since their relinquishment of them (see Table 6.3). Some
gave the adoptee a family heirloom. Many had kept baby mementoes. Others
had registered with the Adoption Disclosure Register. These symbolic gestures of concern for their relinquished children strengthened the image of
the birth mother's relinquishment as an unselfish act performed for the
adoptee's benefit. As such, these gestures gave the adoptee encouragement
for a positive adoptee–birth mother relationship. One claimed, 'I didn't feel
anything when I met her. I thought, "This is a stranger!" I really had a
lot of trouble feeling an attachment. But she asked if I would like to meet
again. I agreed. Like, the night we met, she had saved a music box for
me that was her mother's. She told me, "It would have been your grandmother's. I kept it for you." I thought that it couldn't have been easy for
her. I thought that it was worth the effort to try and become friends' (female,
age 29). Another said, 'Before, I sort of thought that she had a kid and
decided, "Let's get rid of it." There was a little bit of hate there against
her. But, then I found out the reasons. We sat and talked. She let me ask
any questions that I wanted. Like, the only thing that she had of me was
my identification bracelet from the hospital. She gave it to me the first
day I was there. Then, I knew that it was hard for her. She asked if I
wanted to keep it. I said, "No, you have had it so long that you should
keep it." Besides, I knew that I was coming back. For both of us' (male,
age 24).

By supporting the image of a birth mother who has been hurt emotionally
by the relinquishment of her child, these symbolic gestures revoked the 'unchosen child' message incorporated in adoption and affirmed the adoptee's
definition of self as a child who was valued by the birth mother. Thus,
these adoptees continued contact with the birth mother because they believed
their contact held meaning for her. As one woman with a birth mother
who was 'not in very good circumstances' explained, 'I was in shock when
I actually went to see her because I hadn't been used to anything like that.
The screen door was off the hinges. They had no running water. They were
living in poverty. But you had to give the lady credit for guts to level with

TABLE 6.2
Adoptees' description of established relationship (rounded to nearest per cent) ($N = 38$)

Type of reunion	Males		Females		Total	
	N	%	N	%	N	%
One meeting	3	27	1	4	4	11
Disengaged	1	9	5	19	6	16
Limited contact	0	0	4	15	4	11
Duty	1	9	5	19	6	16
Friendship	3	27	9	33	12	32
Mother–child	3	27	3	11	6	16
Total	11	99	27	101	38	102
	(29%)		(71%)		(100%)	

everybody at that point in her life. Nobody knew about me and she told them. She was introducing me to her friends and her neighbours as her daughter. It meant something to her. So, I kept up contact. I mean, if she wants it, I'll go for it. I mean, I started the whole thing. She isn't such a bad person. She's just had bad times' (female, age 39). This scenario contrasts with the decision made by a 'rejecting' adoptee who described his contact situation saying, 'Every other word was a swear word. You could tell she was rough. She didn't ask me anything about myself. I got this sob story about how her husband beat her and he wouldn't work. Then, out of the blue, she said, "Don't ask me about your father because I was raped and I can't tell you." I hadn't even asked her or anything. There was no lead up to it or anything. The way she just dropped it out of the blue. She didn't care much about my feelings to say that without any preparation. I decided, then, that I had enough. I walked out' (male, age 24). Unlike the 'accepted' birth mother who demonstrated her feelings for the adoptee by revealing her birth mother status to others, this 'rejected' birth mother revealed her apparent lack of interest in the adoptee's welfare with an insensitive announcement of her rape. This adoptee perceived this disclosure as a reflection of this woman's character as a selfish and uncaring birth mother. When he combined this self-centred attitude with the birth mother's social situation, he severed contact.

These types of examples demonstrate how the birth mother's actions may affect the outcome of contact. If her behaviour supports the motherhood myth of a disreputable birth mother who cares little for her birth child, then, the adoptee is likely to sever contact. If, as in 'disengaged' reunions,

TABLE 6.3
Symbolic gesture and type of contact (rounded to nearest per cent) (N = 38)

Gesture	Limited contact		Duty		Friends		Mother–child		Total	
	N	%	N	%	N	%	N	%	N	%
Tried to keep adoptee	2	40	1	25	2	13	1	7	6	16
Gave memento	1	20	1	25	8	53	7	50	17	45
Searched	1	20	0	0	1	7	1	7	3	8
Told others	1	20	2	50	4	27	5	36	12	32
Total	5	100	4	100	15	100	14	100	38	101

she gives the impression that she fears disclosure, then the adoptee is likely to wait for her to re-establish contact. If she negates the unchosen child story through symbolic gestures of continued concern or an open response to the adoptee's need for more background information, then the adoptee is likely to begin the difficult process of developing an adoptee–birth mother relationship.

Of particular note in discussing outcomes of the contact is the adoptees' failure to ask the birth mother for an account of her behaviour. As mentioned previously, 'rejected,' 'disengaged,' 'limited contact,' and 'rejecting' adoptees assign their own vocabulary of motives to the behaviour of the birth mother upon contact. In contrast, the candid dialogue established in 'open' contact supports the development of a long-term adoptee–birth mother relationship. Like those adoptees involved in other types of contact, however, 'open' adoptees avoid confrontations with the birth mother that might resolve some of the tension produced by her relinquishment of them. They assign, also, their own vocabulary of motives to her behaviour upon contact. In this way, the adoptees' perception of the birth mother's contact needs also affects the dynamics of their behaviour towards her.

LONG-TERM CONTACT, NEGOTIATION OF ROLES, AND THE DEVELOPMENT OF AN ADOPTEE–BIRTH MOTHER RELATIONSHIP

Despite both the birth mother's and the adoptee's desire for continued contact, the development of a contact relationship is a demanding process. The lack of normative guidelines for adoptee–birth mother interactions creates a 'struggle for role identity' (Stoneman et al., 1980: 10) that requires constant negotiation as the number of meetings between the adoptee and the birth mother increase. The twenty-four adoptees who continued long-term contact describe three distinct types of contact: 'duty' (six or 25 per cent), 'friendship' (twelve or 50 per cent) and 'parent–child' (six or 25 per cent). For example, one man described his 'parent–child' relationship as 'just as close as any mother and son. We talk on the phone two or three times a week. I think that once I met her, the relationship was established. I got that feeling that we would have a relationship. The good feelings were there. We were both able to communicate that right away' (male, age 54).

In contrast, another male noted that his adoptee–birth mother 'friendship' consisted of 'visits mostly. The visits are nice. But you drive there for an hour and you sit and talk. That's basically what we do. You don't get out and camp or hike or things like that because of the distance. So, our friendship and getting to know one another is more on a conversational basis than a companionship. We talk about anything that you would sit down and talk to friends about. Your life, your plans, your children. Things like that' (male, age 34). A third male involved in 'duty' contact claimed, 'I wouldn't even call it a relationship. I go over there from time to time and just drop in for a visit with her and sit down and have a cup of tea. She's not a big one for conversation. I have to sit and drag it out of her. Being a shy person, myself, I find it hard. It takes a lot of work. I find at times that we're just sitting there. You have to feel out the situation. You can't just go in and say, "Well, here's a cup of tea, now spill your guts." You have to feel it out. I guess she just doesn't want to talk much' (male, age 35).

In this way, the adoptees' response to the birth mother's demeanour, her life situation and, her own interactional style affect their negotiation of a satisfactory adoptee–birth mother relationship.

Duty Contact

Adoptees in 'duty' contacts presented the most dramatic example of this role-negotiation process. Six (25 per cent) 'open contact' adoptees maintained contact with the birth mother out of a 'sense of duty' to her. These six adoptees found a birth mother 'so different from me in her upbringing and her lifestyle that it is hard to find a common ground' for continued interaction. They maintained contact mainly because 'she wants it. I don't think that I could ever cut it off unless she wanted to. I just can't hurt somebody like that. To make contact and just drop it when she seems to want it and need it. It just doesn't seem fair. So, I still keep in touch' (female, age 29).

These 'duty' adoptees compare significantly with the 'rejecting' adoptees in this study. Both groups found a woman who was 'on welfare,' 'sexually promiscuous,' and 'lower class.' However, unlike those birth mothers who paid little attention to the 'rejecting' adoptees' needs for contact, however, the birth mothers in 'duty' relationships demonstrated a loving attitude towards the adoptee and a desire for continued contact. For this reason, one of the 'duty' adoptees said, 'I will always maintain some kind of contact. I feel very sorry for her. Like after the first time that I met her, I was happy with that. I didn't want further contact. I had gotten a lot of family history. I was content. I did not want to disturb her life. She looked like a woman who did not have a handle on life. I thought that she must have had a terrible life to get herself so run down. She's on welfare and she's slovenly. But, a while later, I got this call from the Children's Aid office that she was looking for me. I called her. We talked on the phone every day for a while. We met again. Every time that she saw me, she would tell me that she loved me. That she had always loved me. That was so nice to hear. She has shown me how important I am to her' (female, age 38).

Regardless of their apparent distress at the birth mother's current life situation, standards of behaviour, or moral ethics, 'duty' adoptees received positive rewards from their adoptee–birth mother interactions. The birth mother's loving attitude counterbalanced the 'unchosen child' message underlying her relinquishment of them. Those expressions of love and concern restricted the interactions of four 'duty' adoptees who found birth mothers who insisted on performing the 'mother' role. At the same time, these birth mothers ignored the primacy of the adoptive parent–child relationship and the adoptees' experience within the adoptive family structure. This behaviour of the birth mother suggested an intimacy and familiarity unreciprocated by these adoptees. Because they could not bring their full identity to their adoption–birth mother interactions, they were uncomfortable in her presence. This pretence awareness context contributed to their definition of contact as 'duty'. As one woman remarked, 'She had got her baby back and she wasn't letting me go. I said to her, "Take a look at me! Look at what a wonderful job my parents did with me. They were fantastic people. See how they raised me." She still said, "But you're mine." I just sort of wanted to be a friend. She wouldn't let me. I think that we call each other about once a month because she lives so far. But I find it hard. It's eased up. She thinks of me as her daughter. She will never give that up. And I can never accept that. I am not her daughter. I am the daughter of my parents. It's like she thinks all those years went by and they meant nothing' (female, age 42).

Five of the adoptees in 'friendship' contacts found birth mothers who tried to enact the 'mother' role. However, when these 'friendship' adoptees told the birth mother that 'she wasn't my mother, just an important person in my life', the birth mother adjusted her behaviour. This change from a pretence awareness context into an open awareness context eased the tension of future adoptee–birth mother contacts. In this way, these adoptees could bring their full identity to their adoptee–birth mother interactions and negotiate a more satisfactory 'friendship' contact. A member of this group described this situation, saying, 'It was tense at the beginning. She just kind of sucked me up. She tried to become a mother. I can understand her point. Like, "My God. Here's my lost child. I've found her." And, she's very nurturing as a person. I had to make her realize my age and my position. That, she doesn't have to nurture me. That, she had to see me as a friend. That's something she finds hard. She keeps trying. It gets better and easier every time. We are slowly becoming friends' (female, age 42).

Three 'duty' adoptees attempted similar, but unsuccessful, confrontations. These women resisted the role of 'friend' because they perceived themselves as 'mother.' Thus, they viewed contact as a reunification of their biological family and were not going to change their behaviour. The birth mothers' smothering attitude towards these adoptees and their apparent lack of concern for the adoptive parents' position in the adoptees' lives reflect that definition of the situation. In this way, the birth mother's own needs for contact dominated the adoptee–birth mother process negotiating roles. Although it made for a tense and demanding process of social interaction, these 'duty' adoptees accepted this definition of contact because it affirmed their value as a relinquished 'birth child' who was still cared for by its birth mother.

Friendship Contact

Although the majority of searching adoptees envision a friendship with the birth mother (Sachdev, 1992: 63), only half (twelve or 50 per cent) of the long-term contact adoptees in this study described their adoptee–birth mother interactions as 'friendly,' 'warm,' 'close,' 'companionable,' and 'affectionate.' These 'friendship' contacts had developed slowly over time as both birth mother and adoptee became more aware of, and comfortable with, the other's identity. However, unlike other social relationships, the reasons for initiating adoptee–birth mother contact placed extra strain on that interaction process. One of the 'friendship' adoptees outlined the stages required in the development of this contact type. He advised,

A person must go very slowly and cautiously. And wait. See how it works. For me, first there was meeting the person for the first time and not knowing what to say. Or, how to say it. After that, if the relationship is going to work into something, then, you start talking a little more about other things that maybe you wouldn't tell anybody else. Getting closer. Getting to know the other person better. Because, the first step is just finding out the answers to your questions. The next stage is finding out about each other. After you get to know the person a bit more, then, maybe you may want to get into a relationship of mother–son, or just friends. You can decide if it's going to work after you get to know the person. Her likes and dislikes. They may not mix with yours. If you are compatible or not. If you talk about your differences, then, it's okay. From there, you just take it one step at a time. Slowly and cautiously. Like any other relationship that you get into' (male, age 24).

In contrast with 'duty' contact, these 'friendship' adoptees found their adoptee–birth mother interactions surrounded by an open awareness context. The birth mother responded willingly to their questions and, often, provided information without prodding. She recognized the adoptees' full identity and respected the adoptive parents' central position in their lives. This open attitude eased the tension of contact with the birth mother. Unlike 'duty' adoptees, 'friendship' adoptees could openly discuss their past experiences, their future plans, and their current life events without fear of the birth mother's possible negative reaction. In addition, these adoptees found other ways to relate to the birth mother. They fostered their 'friendship' contact through a corresponding taste in books, involvement in sporting activities, a similar pursuit of occupational goals, and so forth. These other interests diverted the strong emotions created by relinquishment and the strain produced from an enactment of an artificial parent–child role. These common interests recast the process of role negotiation in their adoptee–birth mother interactions to a form that supported 'friendship' contact. As one woman explained, 'In some ways, we are so alike that it makes it easier to be together. We both like country music. At first, I used to go to visit her and she would put on her tapes and we'd sit and talk and listen to music. It was like being teenagers. We talked about everything and anything that popped into our heads. In that way, we became friends' (female, age 36).

The descriptions of the process of role negotiation involved in 'friendship' contact support the description of 'disengaged' adoptees who claim little distress over the birth mother's withdrawal from continued contact. Once adoptees have their questions answered, they have less need to meet with their birth mothers. Unless the birth mother or the adoptee gain some positive reward from contact, or find other reasons to interact, disengagement is a strong possibility. Disengagement may result, therefore, from both the adoptees' and the birth mothers' inability to bridge the gap of time and social experience existing between relinquishment and reunion. If both parties have achieved their objectives, then, there may be little reason for further interaction. The assurance of possible future contact may be all that either party needs. Interviews with more adoptees and birth mothers involved in 'disengagement' contacts are needed, however, to explore this hypothesis further.

Parent–Child Contact

Six 'open contact' (25 per cent) adoptees engaged in 'parent–child' interactions. Although these adoptees had not expected or desired this type of contact, they experienced an immediate feeling of intimacy with the birth mother at their first face-to-face meeting. Also, as in 'friendship' contact, the birth mother created an open awareness context around their adoptee–birth mother interactions. She willingly answered all of the adoptees' questions, acknowledged his or her adoptive experience, and respected the adoptive parents' primary position in the adoptee's life. These 'parent–child' contacts began, therefore, as 'friendship' contacts. Gradually, over time, the relationship evolved into a 'parent–child' relationship. Thus, one man engaged in 'parent–child' contact explained, 'I think that once I met her the relationship was established by the feelings that we seemed to have for each other. The respect for each other's position, you might say. I got the feeling that we would have a close relationship. But, then, I just relaxed and let it come by itself. Slowly. The good feelings were there. We were both able to communicate that right away. We got just as close as mother and son. I don't think that a mother and son could be any closer' (male, age 54).

FREQUENCY AND TYPE OF ADOPTEE–BIRTH MOTHER CONTACT

Table 6.4 indicates the type and frequency of contact maintained by these adoptees with their birth mothers. No significant pattern exists between frequency of contact and type of contact. Although 'duty' adoptees report tense contact, they, like 'parent–child' adoptees communicate with the birth mother mainly on holidays and special occasions. 'Duty' adoptees telephone the birth mother also to demonstrate their concern for her or to give her news about their personal lives. Thus, for example, one 'duty' adoptee saw

TABLE 6.4
Type and frequency of contact maintained between birth mother and adoptee
(rounded to nearest per cent) (N = 94)

Contact frequency	Telephone		Letters		Visits		Total	
	N	%	N	%	N	%	N	%
Weekly	12	43	1	4	2	5	15	16
2-3 times/month	4	14	3	11	9	24	16	17
Special occasions	12	43	24	86	17	45	53	56
Stopped after 3-4 meetings	-	-	-	-	6	16	6	6
Stopped after 1 meeting	-	-	-	-	4	11	4	4
Total	28	100	28	101	38	101	94	99

his birth mother at least once a week because she lived in the same community as he. In contrast, a 'parent–child' adoptee visited her birth mother once a year because she lived in a different province. Contact appears to be affected more, therefore, by distance, cost, and time. One 'friendship' adoptee remarked, 'The only thing that I can say that is negative is that we don't get together enough. That's only because our lives are so busy. Who's got time to run around? You already have two sets of parents with your in-laws. Now, there's three sets of parents to visit. Where do you find all the time? Plus, the time to do other things, too. The house, the yard, our friends. Really, it's very hard to find time for everything as it is' (male, age 34).

This pattern of contact is consistent with the findings of both Sachdev (1992) and Pacheco and Eme (1993: 61), who report the 'most common current pattern being monthly/bimonthly or holidays.' After the initial face-to-face meeting, there is an intense period of mutual contact that tapers off into more regular intervals (Depp, 1982; Gonyo and Watson, 1988; Pacheco and Eme, 1993; Sachdev, 1992; Silverman et al., 1988; Sorosky et al., 1978; Stoneman et al., 1985; Thompson, 1978). This initial period of intensity stems from the adoptees' desire to gain more background information. However, because additional adoptee-birth mother contact transmits further information about the adoptee's genetic background and the birth mother's personal situation in life, each additional contact may weaken or strengthen the desire for an adoptee–birth mother relationship. As previously mentioned, those adoptees who maintain contact must find some other reason than fact-finding if they are to continue their adoptee–birth mother relationship. Continuation of contact produces, in turn, a social history that may also be used to close the gap of time and experience since relinquishment. One such 'parent–child' adoptee described her contact relationship, saying, 'I think we have a mother-daughter relationship of a different sort. Like, just the fact that I don't call her mother. Stuff like that. But, she came to my wedding. She was there when my kids were born. She's in my life. I talk to her about her job. And my job. About her stepchildren and her husband's ex-wife. I'll talk to her and tell her this and that. And, she'll tell me this and that. We share things' (female, age 31). Over the years, this woman had developed a series of positive interactions with her birth mother that made each a part of the other's biography and a central figure in the other's life.

SEEKING THE OTHER HALF THROUGH CONTACT WITH THE BIRTH FATHER

Studies on the search for and contact with the birth mother focus little on the topic of birth fathers (Gonyo and Watson, 1988: 19; McWhinnie, 1967; Sorosky et al., 1974, 1975, 1978; Stoneman et al., 1980; Thompson et al., 1978; Triseliotis, 1973). Although this neglect of birth fathers is understandable in light of the general disregard of fathers in the family literature (Eichler, 1988), it stems mainly from the birth mother's dominant position in the adoption process. Until recently, the birth father's permission was not required for relinquishment of the child for adoption. In addition, the birth mother was the one person consistently present at the adoptee's conception, birth, and relinquishment. Adoptees express little interest, therefore, in the birth father when they begin to search (Simpson et al., 1981; Sobol and Cardiff, 1985). For example, one of the adoptees in this study noted that 'the father is different than the mother. The mother carried you for nine months. She means more to you. The father. He has no real physical connection to you. Mine. His family wasn't even aware that he had a child. I don't think I thought of him much until after I began to search' (female, age 35).

These adoptees had expressed little interest in the identity of the birth father during their search. Like other searchers (Sachdev, 1992), their childhood fantasies focused primarily on the birth mother, and their search efforts were directed mainly towards finding her. Their interest in the birth father increased as they gathered and absorbed more background information through their search for their birth mother. Thoughts of contact with their birth father emerged, therefore, at some point in the search or, shortly after contact with the birth mother. In this way, contact with the birth father became an additional stage of the process of contact with the birth mother.

To quote one man, 'The background information that I got gave me more positive feelings towards him than I had before my search. Finding him just seemed like an opportunity to make things more complete. Especially when I found out that they had a relationship for over two years. That he had cared about her. And taken care of her during the pregnancy' (male, age 30).

Data on contact with birth fathers became available in this study mainly because these adoptees had experienced enough time since contact with the birth mother to commit themselves to a possible adoptee–birth father relationship. These adoptees realized that contact with the birth father involved a second search. Because that second search required similar search preparation, obsession with the search, and commitment to the contact as did the first (birth mother) search, they needed time to prepare for that possibility. In particular, they needed time to process the background of their birth mother and the outcome of the contact before considering contact with the birth father. One woman replied, 'I found her at Christmas. It wasn't until the next May that I began to search for him. She gave me his name right away but I didn't want to proceed any further. I just didn't. It had never crossed my mind to look for him. I was all wrapped up in her. Then, one day, I started to think about him. I decided to search for him. Like, I wanted to see her at once. He came later. He was a bonus. That's how I think of him, (female, age 37). Another woman explained, 'It took me about six or seven years before I began to search for my father. It took that long to gather up all the information that I wanted about my mother. I remember sitting there and talking and I thought that I should look for him. So, it wasn't because of her rejection. It was more a second step for me. I don't know how some people feel, but I wanted to know something about him. I realized how much I was like my mother, but I thought that there must be something from him too. Because, he also had a hand in it' (female, age 55).

Like the search for the birth mother, the stages involved in the decision to search for the birth father, gather background information, and initiate contact with him depended upon the adoptees' ability to gain access to data on the birth father and absorb it as a part of self. However, their previous experience with the search for the birth mother influenced the transition from one stage of the search to the next. For example, the majority of these adoptees needed considerable time to process the data on their birth mother and the outcome of the contact with their birth mother before they decided to search for their birth father. Others discarded the idea when they received negative information about their birth father during the search for their birth mother. Some used a search for the birth father to resolve their sense of rejection by the birth mother's response to contact. Many wished merely to learn about the 'other half.'

The adoptee–birth mother contact relationship complicated the process of searching for the birth father. For example, seven (88 per cent) of the eight 'rejected' adoptees in this study expressed an interest in a search for the birth father but could not proceed because they received no information on him from the birth mother (see Tables 6.5 and 6.6). Over half (56 per cent) of the 'disengaged' adoptees expressed an interest, also, in contact with the birth father, but the birth mother would not discuss his identity. Thus, one 'rejected' adoptee said, 'I wrote her a letter. She phoned back a few weeks later. She was cold. I got the impression she just wanted me to disappear. When I asked her what the birth father's name was, she answered, "You find him the same way you found me." I was so stunned by her response that I should have pointed out that I had her name and that's how I found her. That I couldn't find him because I needed her to give me his name. But she asked that I not contact her again and hung up' (female, age 43). And, a 'disengaged' adoptee reported, 'I asked her about the father. She said, "I refuse to mention it to my dying day. That information is locked deeply in my heart." I'm really disappointed because I would like to know who he is. Where he is. What he's like. Because he's part of me too. But she took it personally when I pushed it. She said, "That's all you wanted to meet me for was to find him." She was upset about that. I couldn't convince her otherwise. I never got another chance because she refused to see me after that meeting' (male, age 42).

In contrast, the majority of 'conditional contact' and 'open contact' adoptees received the birth mother's support for contact with the birth father. One said, 'I asked her for the name of my father. She gave it to me right out. She wrote it down for me and said that she didn't know if he was still living in the area because she had no contact with him after me. That he had a large family in the area and she had no reason to believe that he had left. She had no bitterness toward him. She said that she cared for him a lot' (male, age 25). In this way, the birth mother's dominant position in the adoption process may affect the dynamics of the search for and contact with the birth father. Only she possesses certain knowledge of the birth father's identity. If she is willing to identify him or supply accurate background information, she can facilitate the search for and contact with the birth father. However, if she refuses to identify the birth father, she can block the adoptee's search for him.

In a similar fashion, the birth mother's attitude towards, and description

TABLE 6.5

Type of contact with birth mother and interest in contact with birth father (rounded to nearest per cent) (N = 60)

Type of contact	No		Interested but has not searched		In search		Has contact		Birth father deceased		Total	
	N	%	N	%	N	%	N	%	N	%	N	%
Rejected	1	8	5	25	0	0	1	6	1	17	8	13
Disengaged	1	8	4	20	0	0	3	19	1	17	9	15
Rejects birth mother	1	8	2	10	1	20	3	19	0	0	7	12
Conditional limited contact	1	8	3	15	1	20	1	6	1	17	7	12
Duty	3	23	1	5	0	0	2	13	0	0	6	10
Friends	4	31	1	5	0	0	4	25	3	50	12	20
Mother–child	2	15	0	0	3	60	1	6	0	0	6	10
Birth mother deceased	0	0	4	20	0	0	1	6	0	0	5	8
Total	13	101	20	100	5	100	16	100	6	101	60	100
	(22%)		(33%)		(8%)		(27%)		(10%)		(100%)	

TABLE 6.6
Type of contact and birth mother's description of birth father
(rounded to nearest per cent) ($N = 55$)

Type of contact	Positive		Negative		Will not discuss		Total	
	N	%	N	%	N	%	N	%
Rejected	0	0	0	0	8	100	8	100
Disengaged	4	44	0	0	5	56	9	100
Rejecting	2	29	3	43	2	29	7	101
Conditional contact	4	57	0	0	3	43	7	100
Duty	4	67	0	0	2	33	6	100
Friends	7	58	3	25	2	17	12	100
Mother–child	2	33	2	33	2	33	6	99
Total	23	43	8	15	24	43	55	101

Note: The five adoptees who found their birth mother deceased have been eliminated from this table.

of the birth father may influence the adoptee's search decision. For example, four (57 per cent) of the seven 'conditional contact' adoptees and thirteen (54 per cent) of the twenty-four 'open contact' adoptees received a positive description of the birth father and his relationship with the birth mother. In five cases, the birth mother approached the birth father and arranged a meeting for the adoptee. When these birth mothers supplied information about the birth father, they removed the element of secrecy in adoption. They created an open awareness context around their adoptee–birth mother interactions that strengthened their own continued outcome of contact. Because these adoptees perceived their birth mothers' behaviour as a recognition of their needs for contact and a symbol of her regard for them they desired more interaction with her. As a result, nine (38 per cent) of the twenty-four 'open contact' and one (14 per cent) of the seven 'conditional contact' adoptees were in agreement with the explanation of one, who said, 'I have no interest in a reunion with him. She was very open about him. He was Roman Catholic. In those days you just didn't marry out of the church and her father was very strict. She loved him dearly but she never even told him about me. She's kept track of him over the years. Sometimes, I have this urge to go down and just take a look at him. But she said that he's a real nice man who loved her and loved children and animals and all that. I get any information that I want about him from her. So, I don't need to meet him' (female, age 43). And another adoptee with similar views said, 'I have no urge to meet him. She answered most of my questions to the best of her knowledge. I would say that a good 80 or 90 per cent of the questions that I did have of him, she answered. I accept her answers. And she would rather that I didn't look for him. I respect that. Because he's a jerk. He got her pregnant and another girl at the same time. He abandoned her. Finding him could disrupt our lives. Both hers and mine' (male, age 24). Thus, it was not the birth mother's description of the birth father that led these adoptees to seek contact. Rather, it was the relationship that they had developed with her and their perception of the birth father's intrusion into her life.

Those adoptees with unresponsive birth mothers found themselves, once again, in the powerless position created by secrecy in adoption. Once again, they were at the mercy of another person who refused to disclose to them information about themselves. These adoptees had expected that, as a member of the adoption triangle, the birth mother would understand, and comply with, their request regarding their birth father. They felt betrayed, therefore, by her denial of their needs for contact with him. One of these adoptees said, 'It's like another rejection. I only asked her for one thing in my life. She might not think that it is important but I asked her for my father's name. She said, "You want it. You get it. Find him the same way you found me." She hung up. After forty years, if my daughter phoned up, I certainly would have given her a few scraps. It's a part of my life that only she can tell me about. I didn't think that was too much to ask for. I guess she did. It's funny. You would think that one biological tie would be enough. But I need that one too. So, I'm really disappointed. And angry. At her. That she couldn't even give me that' (female, age 39). Another re-marked, 'I was pretty mad at her for a while. There was a period of about three years when we would have constant fights over that. I wanted to find him. She wouldn't give me his name. It was only after constant nagging and persistence that she finally gave in. I had to have it. I guess because he is the other part of me that I didn't know' (female, age 42).

Few adoptees confronted the birth mother so vehemently. The majority found that their commitment to the birth mother's privacy restricted their demands. They feared, also, that, if they pushed too hard, the birth mother might disengage from contact. The position of power given to her in the contact situation and its outcome left them vulnerable to such requests. Thus, one 'limited contact' adoptee explained, 'I dropped the subject. I wasn't quite satisfied with her answers about him. Yet, I have to be. She gets upset whenever the subject is mentioned. So, I have to let it go. Or we might never be able to talk at all. She could cut me off entirely' (female, age 53).

Birth mothers who obstructed access to information about the birth father destroyed the possibility of an open awareness context in their adoptee–birth mother interactions. Some birth mothers formed pretence awareness contexts by avoiding the topic. Thus, one 'limited contact' adoptee stated, 'I asked her for my birth father's name. She says she can't remember. It's strange. She says he was tall and fair-haired. She can remember that but she can't remember who he was. But what do you do? You can't press it. I can't understand it. That should be first and foremost in her mind. It really bothers me. Even, if it was a nightmare. I know that she was seventeen and tried to block it out. But, not remembering? It's hard to believe' (female, age 48).

Other birth mothers formed suspicion awareness contexts when they offered false descriptions of the birth father. For example, one woman described the contact with her birth mother as 'uncomfortable,' saying, 'She told me this story about my birth father being her husband. They were separated and had a reunion of sorts. I was the product of that reunion. When he found out she was pregnant, he left her. But she told Social Services a different story. And the dates don't match. So, I don't believe her. It makes me wonder what else I can believe, (female, age 45).

These accounts of the birth mother's closed attitude towards the birth father support Sachdev's report (1992: 62) that 'most biological mothers (80.4 per cent) did not wish to discuss the biological father.' The identity of the birth father may have more impact, therefore, on the birth mother's decision regarding contact than adoptees believe. Adoptees enter the search with the need to resolve their biographical discontinuities through contact with their birth mother. They perceive the birth mother mainly as a resource person who has direct access to their genetic and genealogical background. Their desire for contact with their birth father supports that perception. Because their background originates with two biological parents, they view contact with the birth father as their search for the 'other half.'

The birth mother may not view contact in this manner. She may perceive the adoptee's contact as a fulfilment of her own desires to resolve the pain of her relinquishment through a renewed connection with her 'lost' child. This factor has arisen in other research studies on the searching behaviour of birth mothers. For example, in their study of search by birth parents, Silverman et al. (1988: 525) noted that, at the time of relinquishment, 'many birth mothers felt coerced into agreeing they could/should not keep the baby,' and most birth mothers 'saw no alternative' but relinquishment of their child. Furthermore, the lack of information about what happened to their baby and the strong feelings of attachment and separation experienced by these birth mothers caused a 'grief after the surrender worse than anticipated. Some birth parents mentioned feeling suicidal' (Silverman et al., 1988: 525). As a result, even though contact may help birth mothers resolve some of these emotions through knowledge of the adoptee's life, it may also reactivate memories of the pain and personal humiliation described in Silverman et al.'s study. If the birth father did not support the birth mother, she may experience great anger towards him. These birth mothers may view the adoptee's request for information about the birth father, therefore, as a betrayal of their own needs from the contact and a disregard for the pain that they experienced from their relinquishment. Further study of the birth mothers' perception of reunion contact is necessary, however, to assess this situation adequately.

CONTACT WITH THE BIRTH FATHER

Twenty-two (37 per cent) of the adoptees in this study conducted searches for their birth father and made contact with him. The results of those searches spanned the same range of contact types as reported for birth mothers (see Table 6.7). 'Disengaged contact' was the only type of contact not reported. However, absence of this type of contact is likely to be a product of the small number of birth father searches completed by this sample than the inability to form such contacts. In addition, the small body of knowledge on contact with the birth father makes comparison with other studies impossible (Griffith, 1991: Section 5: 8) and the reliability and validity of these reports questionable.

Those adoptees who experienced contact with the birth father described types of contact that matched the descriptions given for the outcomes of contact with the birth mother. However, outcomes of contact with the birth mother were not related significantly to the type of adoptee–birth father relationship established. For example, one woman who engaged in a 'friendship' contact with her birth mother experienced 'disengagement' with her birth father. She explained that 'he met me at my home. He brought all kinds of pictures of his family and everything. That's the only time that I saw him. He told me that it wasn't indifference. That he did think about me but his family didn't know. I agreed. What was needed was accomplished. He knows that I am alive and well. I have a bit of information on him. That was enough for both of us' (female, age 38). In a similar way, a young man who encountered rejection by his birth mother claimed that he had difficulty with his birth father's desire for 'parent–child' contact. He said, 'When we met, he was very emotional. He wanted to touch me and know

TABLE 6.7
Contact with birth father (rounded to nearest per cent) ($N = 22$)

Type of contact	Males		Females		Total	
	N	%	N	%	N	%
Rejected	1	17	1	6	2	9
Disengaged	0	0	0	0	0	0
Rejecting	0	0	1	6	1	5
Duty	0	0	2	13	2	9
Limited contact	1	17	1	6	2	9
Friends	2	33	4	25	7	32
Father–child	1	17	1	6	2	9
Birth father deceased	1	17	6	38	6	27
Total	6	101	16	100	22	100

everything about me. To bring me back to meet his family. It was over-whelming. I thought, "God, you want me for a son." I was scared that he expected me to be his son and move in. That I should call him all the time. "Later," I told him. He said that I didn't have to feel that way. He said, "I want you to be a part of my family but I don't want to scare you away. I don't want to smother you. If you call me, I'm here." Then, it got easier because I called him because I wanted to not because I felt like I had to' (male, age 25).

Thus, the pattern of contact with the birth father matches that of contact with the birth mother. Adoptees must negotiate their adoptee–birth father interactions in a similar manner as they negotiate their adoptee–birth mother interactions. Open, pretence, or suspicion awareness contexts may surround those interactions as well. However, the experience of search for the birth mother and contact with her may prepare adoptees for their interactions with birth fathers by relieving some of the tension and shock of meeting a 'stranger.' It may also give them a stronger understanding of their own expectations of contact. What it cannot do is prepare adoptees for the birth father's own response to contact. Like the birth mother, the birth father has his own agenda that must be considered. As occurred in contact with birth mothers, the adoptee and his or her birth father must acquaint them-selves with each other and negotiate their own adoptee–birth father in-teractions. The accounts presented in this study reveal the need for a more extensive examination of this specific role relationship for, as these adoptees indicate, once contact with the birth mother occurs, the desire for contact with the birth father soon follows.

Face-to-face contact with the birth mother established, with great clarity, the birth mother's role as the source of the adoptee's genealogical and genetic heritage. Yet the gap of time and social experience between relinquishment of the child and contact with the birth mother had weakened the power of the biological bond and the impact of the background information conveyed by her. These adoptees met with a 'stranger' whom they had to get to know. This perception reinforced their view of themselves as the product of their adoptive parents' influence. For this reason, adoptees accepted disengagement of contact with the birth mother, limited contact with the birth mother, and opposing lifestyles of the birth mother more easily. Their original search goal had been achieved and they could put their contact experience behind them.

The birth mother's willingness to disclose genealogical information, details on the adoptee's conception, birth, and relinquishment, and information on the birth father affected outcome of the contact. Although the birth mother's behaviour is difficult to assess without verification through interviews with her, twenty-four adoptees claimed 'open' contact with their birth mothers. These adoptees described a process of role negotiation in which birth mother and adoptee established the boundaries of their contact relationship. That role negotiation process resulted in three main contact types: 'duty,' 'friendship,' and 'parent–child.' Involvement in a specific type of contact depended greatly upon the birth mother's own contact needs and the adoptees' view of her dominant position of power to determine the outcome of the contact.

The process of the search for and contact with the birth mother increased the desire for more knowledge on the identity of the birth father. The birth mother's dominant position in the adoption process gave her control, however, over the release of information about him. Her openness about the birth father and her willingness to discuss him with the adoptee affected the adoptee–birth mother interaction process. If she surrounded their interactions within closed, pretence, or suspicion awareness contexts, she made contact uncomfortable and filled with tension. Adoptees questioned her motivations for contact and the validity of her expressed concern for them.

Those adoptees who received incomplete, false, or no information about their birth fathers expressed 'disappointment,' 'regret,' 'great frustration,' 'disillusionment,' and 'anger' at the birth mother's behaviour. This situation created a renewed sense of powerlessness over their adoptive status and the demands of non-disclosure. In addition, the birth mother's apparent lack of interest in their contact needs reactivated the 'unchosen' child message implied by her relinquishment of them. These adoptees explained their birth mother's behaviour, therefore, with the motive talk used to support her need for confidentiality. In this way, their perception of the birth mother's position of power to determine the parameters of adoptee–birth mother contact and their concern over their intrusion into their birth mother's life kept them from pushing her for more information about their birth father.

Data on contact with the birth father became available in this study because these adoptees had experienced enough time since contact with their birth mother to assimilate their findings about her. Twenty-two (37 per cent) of these adoptees searched for their birth fathers, and sixteen (72 per cent) of the twenty-two established contact. These types of contacts with the birth father span the full range of types experienced in contacts with the birth mother. Also, the adoptees' descriptions of adoptee–birth father interaction and outcome of contact resemble the accounts given for contact with the birth mother. This interest in contact with the birth father suggests a topic that should be considered more extensively as an additional stage of the outcome of contact with the birth mother.

7

Completion of Self and Satisfaction with the Contact with the Birth Mother

Regardless of the findings of the search or the birth mother's response to the contact, the adoptees in this study experienced a sense of identity coherence and personal unity upon completion of the search. They filled in the identity 'gaps' produced by non-disclosure and gained knowledge of the events surrounding their conception, birth, and relinquishment. They established, also, with great clarity, their birth parents' role as the source of their genealogical and genetic background and their adoptive parents' role as their primary family relationship. In this way, contact with the birth mother removed these adoptees' doubts about their unknown birth identity at the same time as it supported their identity as adoptees raised within the adoptive family structure.

Studies on contact with the birth mother reveal high levels of satisfaction with the outcome of the contact. The adoptees in this study also reported similar levels of satisfaction from their search and the outcome of the contact with their birth mothers. They linked that sense of satisfaction, however, to their perception of self as more socially acceptable to others after contact with the birth mother. Knowledge of their genetic and genealogical background removed many of the biographical discontinuities created by non-disclosure. That knowledge neutralized the social stigma brought on when their background entered the process of social interaction. These adoptees could now use their newly discovered background information in response to others' curiosity and gain more power over their social interactions. Consequently, regardless of the findings of the search or the outcome of contact, their control over the release of the details surrounding their conception, birth, and relinquishment gave them more satisfactory presentations of self. This new sense of personal power over the process of social interaction influenced the high levels of satisfaction reported by these adoptees when they discussed their search and contact experiences.

SATISFACTION WITH THE OUTCOME OF CONTACT

The majority of reunited adoptees report high levels of satisfaction with their contact with their birth mothers (Anderson, 1989; Depp, 1982; Gonyo and Watson, 1988; Haimes and Timms, 1985; Pacheco and Eme, 1993; Sachdev, 1992; Silverman et al., 1988; Simpson et al., 1981; Sobol and Cardiff, 1983; Sorosky et al., 1974; 1978; Stoneman et al., 1980; Thompson et al., 1978; Triseliotis, 1973). These high levels of satisfaction have little connection, however, with the findings of the search or the outcome of the contact with the birth mother. For example, Pacheco and Eme (1993) observe that 86 per cent of their sample found the reunion to be a positive experience, while 85 per cent said it improved their self-concept, 71 per cent said it improved their self-esteem, and 62 per cent believed it improved their ability to relate to others. In a similar fashion, 85 per cent of Sachdev's sample (1992) were highly or moderately pleased with the outcome of contact and, 94 per cent had no regrets.

The high levels of satisfaction reported in these other studies indicate a positive effect for adoptees from the search for and contact with the birth mother. Yet the lack of a relationship between satisfaction and the findings of the search or the outcome of the contact with the birth mother creates difficulty if one wishes to assess the outcome of reunion in terms of success or failure. As far as adoptees are concerned, even traumatic or negative findings of the search offer a measure of satisfaction to them (Thompson et al., 1978: 28). Thus, it is not the *type* of background information discovered that is significant for adoptees. Rather, it is the *meaning* that this information holds in a society that assesses personal identity and social status on biological kinship ties.

The adoptees in this study reveal a similar sense of satisfaction from contact with their birth mothers. For example, when asked, 'How would you describe a successful reunion,' 86 per cent replied 'mine.' In addition, 95 per cent were 'very satisfied' with the outcome of their contact with the birth mother. These adoptees qualified 'success' and 'satisfaction,' however, in terms of the amount of background information received. Thus, a 're-jecting' adoptee noted, 'My reunion was successful from the point of view that I am satisfied. I found out what I wanted to know. I feel like there is that part of me that was always tugging that is gone. It's relieved. It's finished. I know. There are no more doubts or questions. It was successful from that point of view. That we didn't have a relationship – from that point of view, I guess it was unsuccessful' (female, age 26).

Table 7.1 describes the adoptees' perception of self after contact with

TABLE 7.1
Perception of self after contact with birth mother (rounded to nearest per cent) ($N = 108$)

Perception	First response		Second response		Third response		Total	
	N	%	N	%	N	%	N	%
Relaxed, peaceful	11	18	4	11	3	25	18	17
Complete	21	35	5	14	1	8	27	25
More secure	7	12	9	25	1	8	17	16
Like self better	5	8	5	14	2	17	12	11
Understand self now	1	2	6	17	1	8	8	7
Appreciate adoption	2	3	4	11	4	33	10	9
Angry	2	3	3	8	0	0	5	5
No change	11	18	0	0	0	0	11	10
Total	60	99	36	100	12	99	108	100

their birth mothers. These adoptees were asked the question, 'Do you think that you could take a moment to describe to me the type of person that you were like before your reunion in comparison to the type of person that you are like now?' Twenty-five per cent of the responses to that question referred to the adoptees' sense of being 'more complete' because they have 'filled in the gaps.' Seventeen per cent indicated a feeling of being 'more relaxed and peaceful' because their genetic heritage is no longer in question. Seven per cent referred to a 'better understanding of self' because they can identify the source of certain physical characteristics and personality traits. Thus, one woman replied, 'I'm a lot happier than I was. I always had that blank before. I'm happier now because I know. I know what I am now. She has given me every detail in my background possible. Who died and from what. About my grandparents. She gives me any information that I want' (female, age 42). Another said, 'I'm more relaxed now that I've found out what I need to know. I feel more at peace with myself. Those pieces aren't missing any more. I always thought that I had this big black cloud over me. Now, I feel more complete, (female, age 36).

Five per cent of the responses to this question indicated 'anger and bitterness' over the outcome of their contact experience. Three of the adoptees who replied in this fashion found their 'birth parent deceased.' The other two encountered rejection. These five adoptees linked their anger to the incompleteness of the information obtained through the search. The search had not resolved their sense of powerlessness from non-disclosure and their main search objective had not been achieved. To quote one woman who found her birth mother deceased: 'I still get angry sometimes when I think about it. It's not fair that our roots are closed to us. That the people who brought us into the world are hidden to us. I can vote and travel and get a job. But I can't get information about myself. That bothers me far more than the fact that my birth mother is dead. I can't miss someone that I never knew. So, I wasn't all that sad. I was disappointed that I didn't meet her. I am angry because I should have the same rights as everyone else. I should be able to find out about myself' (female, age 44).

Meeting the birth mother yields more information about one's genealogical and genetic background and permits a more extensive comparison of the contributions of the birth family and the adoptive family to one's own life. Seven of the nine 'no change' responses came, therefore, from adoptees who were denied face-to-face meetings. These adoptees reported little change in self because, as one of them said, 'It's necessary to see her. If you don't get to see her, then, you might as well read a book. You can be satisfied, I guess. I'm satisfied with what I learned. But seeing her in person. That makes her real. It makes the information real too. You can attach it to a real person' (female, age 65).

The adoptees in this study also reported similar identity effects from contact with the birth mother as found in other search and reunion studies. They said that they understood themselves better and had a greater liking for themselves after their search experience. Knowledge of their genetic and genealogical background gave them more confidence and a sense of personal completeness. By gaining access to their background information, these adoptees gained access to those 'hidden' parts of self produced by non-disclosure. This is the major impact of the search for and contact with the birth mother. For this reason, in spite of their search findings or their contact outcome, the majority replied as this adoptee, who noted, 'I am basically the same person. But I have an understanding of where I came from. The reason behind why I was conceived. Why I was born. Why I was adopted. A clear understanding of my background on both sides. Acceptance of myself in accepting my physical attributes and my emotional disposition. Which had always been a burden to me. I had always been ashamed of that before. I still, in some ways, don't accept my lack of control. But I am a lot more comfortable with it. I understand why I am that way now' (female, age 42).

REMOVAL OF BIOGRAPHICAL DISCONTINUITIES

In their description of the effects of contact with their birth mother on self, these adoptees referred continually to the personal identity issues that had led them to search. They mentioned the sense of instability created by their biographical discontinuities and the removal of that sensation once they learned about the events of their conception, birth, and relinquishment. The findings from their search gave them the material needed to create an early biography. In this way, these adoptees related their satisfaction with the search for and contact with the birth mother to the *amount* rather than the *type* of background information discovered. For example, one woman expressed frustration over her lack of knowledge on the first three months of her life. She explained, 'Maybe, it's because I'm an adoptee but I kept baby books for my kids and filled out all the information until they were in grade school. My search fills that gap because there was no baby book for me. But I was three months old when I was adopted. There is no first picture. I can show my kids their pictures and say, "This is you within the first twenty-four hours you were born." There is no gap there. Where, for me, there is the three months where I don't know where I was. In a foster home or what? Nobody seems to be able to answer that. It bothers me. That gap isn't completely filled' (female, age 35).

The majority of these adoptees described the effects of contact with their birth mother in biographical terms. They reported a sense of composing their own story of their beginning as human beings. One noted that 'it's like belonging. Finding her. In a way, I felt like I was writing my own chapter. My story had finally started. After all of these years of wondering. I was finally getting my questions answered. I now know my story and there is no more guessing' (female, age 36).

This sense of 'writing one's own chapter' became apparent as the interview portion of this study progressed. For example, over two-thirds (72 per cent) of these adoptees brought folders, booklets or birth family pictures to the interview session. Five (8 per cent) had kept diaries of their search and reunion experiences. One (2 per cent) had written her story of search and contact for a newspaper article. Six (10 per cent) had saved such souvenirs as coasters, matchbooks, or tourist advertisements taken from the restaurant or motel where they had had their first meeting with their birth mother. This material provided tangible support for statements made to me during their responses to the interview question. These adoptees used this material to create a 'paper identity' or 'permanent and real record' (Haimes and Timms, 1985: 70) of the search for and contact with the birth mother that supported their claims regarding their birth identity.

In this way, the search for and contact with the birth mother gave these adoptees power over the biographical data denied them by non–disclosure. Now, they could place themselves within the biosocial context expected by their society. They had created a biological history for themselves and gained a sense of their own position within the generational context of kinship that others in their society readily possessed. Thus, one man reported, 'I went on a vacation to the place where my birth father came from. I just had to go and look at the land and see what it was like. Where I came from. My roots. Things like that are important to me. I liked the place that I saw. And, the people that I met. You know, it's a small part of me. In an abstract way. Somehow, I'm the result of that. I'm connected with it. Meeting my birth father was some of that as well' (male, age 30).

NEUTRALIZATION OF SOCIAL STIGMA THROUGH CONTACT WITH THE BIRTH MOTHER

In their discussion of the search and their desire for contact, these adoptees claimed a sense of being different because they were adopted. They experienced difficulty meeting others' expectations because their biographical discontinuities prevented them from offering a full account of their biological background. These types of social situations required a revelation of their adoptive status and their 'spoiled' identity as people who were different from the rest (Goffman, 1963). Others' reactions to their accounts of adoption produced unsatisfactory presentations of self and personal doubts about their adoptive identity.

In contrast, the search for and contact with the birth mother removed the biographical discontinuities produced by non-disclosure. It provided adoptees with information on their biological background and the events surrounding their conception, birth, and relinquishment. Search for and contact with birth mothers changed the closed awareness context created by non-disclosure. As a result, these adoptees reported more satisfactory presentations of self after the search for and contact with their birth mothers. They also perceived others as more satisfied with their status as adoptees. The majority, like this adoptee, claimed that 'meeting her put everything into context. All the pieces came together. There was this feeling of actually having been born. Like, I thought I was hatched or something. Here there was a sense of finally being part of a continuum. You are born and you are going to die. It all sort of made sense. I know where I came from, so, I know where I am going. It makes other people happy too. It makes them less concerned about my status because I can give them answers' (female, age 36).

The search for and contact with the birth mother neutralized the effects of the social stigma produced by adoption. It removed the sense of uncertainty about self through the reflected appraisals of others who appeared more satisfied with their biographical accounts. The adoptees did not need continued contact with their birth mothers to achieve this effect. They accomplished their original search goal when they gained the documentary proof needed to anchor self as an object of a complete biography that could be appropriately tested, assessed, and evaluated by others (Goffman, 1963: 62). As one adoptee explained, 'I felt really good that I had beat the system. I had taken control over my own life' (female, age 38). For this reason, 'rejected' adoptees could also say, as one did, 'I am satisfied. It has given me a better insight into myself. Especially, emotion-wise. It has given me a history. It's given me a background. A nationality. And, I guess, if she was different, we might have had a relationship. But, that wasn't what I really set out for anyway. I set out to find out about me. I am satisfied with that' (female, age 45).

Of particular note, here, is the tendency by other research studies to view 'satisfaction' as a uniform concept. As these adoptees illustrate, satisfaction with the search for and contact with the birth mother depends upon the type and extent of background information obtained. Those adoptees who gain continued access to biological background information through open contact with both birth parents experience greater satisfaction than those who do not. Similarly, those adoptees who discover negative background material or birth parents with 'problematic' lifestyles experience disappointment with the results of their search. Few are damaged seriously, however, by the experience. They have resolved their feelings of non-existence prior to adoption and their sense of continuity down through the generations. This resolution is the source of the high levels of satisfaction reported by these adoptees. To quote one of them, 'I think that I feel just more tuned in now. Like, a real, live person. Not different. There is this sense of having been born. You're grounded. So, even if there is no relationship there. There is meaning. Because she gave birth to you and your genes are there. It's your beginning' (female, age 33).

PERCEPTION OF THE ADOPTIVE PARENTS AS THE PRIMARY PARENTS

This ability to complete one's biography establishes, also, an undisputed sense of the adoptive parents' role in the adoptees' formation of self. Other search and reunion studies report that reunited adoptees believe that contact with the birth mother improved their adoptive parent–child relationships (Haimes and Timms, 1985; Pacheco and Eme, 1993; Sachdev, 1992; Sobol and Cardiff, 1983; Sorosky et al., 1974; 1978; Stoneman et al., 1980; Thompson et al., 1978; Triseliotis, 1973). The small samples of adoptive parents in those studies support that belief. The adoptees' relationship with the adoptive parents became closer after the search and some adoptees expressed a stronger appreciation for the greater opportunities received as a result of adoption (Stoneman et al., 1980: 16). This sense of appreciation for their adoptive status stems from the adoptees' ability to place themselves within a biosocial context. As previously mentioned, unlike others in their society, adoptees possess two separate sets of parents who perform distinct roles in their lives. The birth parents provide adoptees with a genealogical and genetic background. The adoptive parents raise their adopted children into adulthood and socialize them to become productive members of their society. Because secrecy in adoption denies adoptees knowledge of the contribution made by their biological parents, the adoptive parents' contribution becomes vague and uncertain, too.

Both Kirk (1964; 1981) and Miall (1986; 1987) discuss the stigma of adoptive parenthood whereby others view the adoptive parent–child bond as weaker than the biological blood bond. In particular, Miall's sample (1987) of seventy-two adoptive mothers perceived that their community considered the birth mother to be their child's authentic mother. These mothers sensed that others believed they could not love their child as strongly as a biological mother could love her child. In addition, these mothers noted that others used their child's biological background to measure his or her worthiness in the larger society and devalued their child for being adopted.

In a similar fashion, the adoptees in this study perceived others' questions about the birth mother's relinquishment and their thoughts about her as support for the primacy of the birth mother–child bond. They noted others' curiosity over the source of particular character traits or physical attributes that distinguished them from their adoptive family members. They experienced a sense of separation, also, from others' references to them as 'the adopted child' or to the birth mother as their 'real' mother. These discriminatory practices cast doubt upon the strength of their adoptive parent–child bonds and their legitimate position within the adoptive family structure.

These adoptees internalized such messages as personal misgivings about self. Furthermore, the constraints of non-disclosure had limited their ability to manage their stigma trait effectively. Their lack of genealogical and genetic information made them uncertain about which parts of self emerged from their biological background, their adoptive parents' child-rearing practices, or as a natural expression of their individuality. By removing the constraints of non-disclosure, the search and contact with the birth mother gave them the ability to 'sort out' these factors. As these adoptees outlined their birth parents' contribution to their development as human beings, they clarified, also, the role played by their adoptive parents in that formation. Thus, for example, a woman involved in 'friendship' contact with her birth mother reported, 'I think that the process has changed me in being more able to understand my parents. Finding out who I am. Now, I can look back and understand why I did certain things. And, I can think that they gave me a lot. Good values. A good education. Who I am now, I owe to them. What they gave me. They did some bad things too, but I realize that this comes with the role of parent. I really appreciate what they did for me' (female, age 42).

One of the greatest difficulties noted in adoptee–birth mother interactions is the problem of 'bridging the gap' of social experience between the time of relinquishment and contact with the birth mother (Gonyo and Watson, 1988; Stoneman et al., 1980). However, by making these adoptees conscious of that gap, contact with the birth mother also accentuated the continuity of experience in their adoptive parent–child relationship. It stressed the years of continued love, mutual interaction, and common social experience existing within their adoptive family structure and clarified the adoptive parents' role as the 'real' parents. The ability to outline these factors made their adoptive-parent child bond stronger after contact with the birth mother. To quote one woman, 'There is a difference. My son. He'll sit there and be doing something and my birth mother will say, "He looks just like M. He reminds me of M. when he was a baby." M. is her son. Now, my mother will say, "Gee, he looks just like you. You used to do that in the same way." Well, my birth mother can't say that about me because she didn't know me then. She doesn't know how I looked or acted when I was a baby. She knows how M. looked or acted because she was there for him. She remembers him. My mother was there for me. She remembers me. That says it all, doesn't it? How can she be my mother? Twenty-eight years of my life have never existed for her, (female, age 33).

Adoptees who experienced the sensation of 'meeting a stranger' through a face-to-face meeting with the birth mother became aware, especially, of this difference. Face-to-face contact clarifies the birth mother's position as the source of certain physical attributes or character traits. It emphasizes, also, the weakness of the biological connection existing between birth mother and child. These adoptees could dismiss, finally, that part of the motherhood myth that supports the birth mother as the 'real' or 'natural' mother. They could put aside the fantasy images produced by non-disclosure and confront the reality of the woman who bore them. As one woman explained, 'Before your reunion, all you are is a phantom. You're not real. Both of you.

All through those years, both of you wonder. The mother knows it has this child and the child knows it has this mother. But, it's not real. You're not real. Then, you meet. All of a sudden, you become real. A successful reunion, it just opens up all these doors. For both parties' (female, age 34).

Because the majority of the adoptees' family life experiences consisted of adoptive parent–child interactions, removal of this phantom image supported these adoptees' perception of self as 'primarily the product of my adoptive parents. They are the ones who played with me and loved me and put the clothes on my back. I never thought of them as anything but my parents. They did more for me than my natural mother or father. Those people did nothing. Only my birth mother has spots to fill in. That's all. That's why I wanted to search. And that's what I found' (female, age 21). These adoptees used this strengthened perception of self as the adoptive parents' child to manage the effects of contact with their birth mother. For example, most 'rejected' adoptees disclaimed a sense of rejection from contact with their birth mother by referring to their close adoptive parent–child bonds. 'Rejecting' adoptees used their adoptive experience to explain their lack of interest in continuing problematic contact with their birth mother. And, 'open contact' adoptees emphasized their adoptive identity during the process of role negotiation involved in their adoptee–birth mother interactions. Thus, one 'friendship' adoptee stated, 'She is not living in very good circumstances. I really didn't care about that. But I was still shocked to meet her. Like, she's one step up from a hooker. I was really amazed that I could take it so calmly. But that was her life, not mine. It really didn't have too much to do with me. I'm different. She made me different. She gave me to my parents and gave me that life and made me different from her. So, she shouldn't complain now that I'm different. She made me that way when she gave me to them' (female, age 39). In a similar fashion, a 'limited contact' adoptee explained, 'She's not a part of my life. I had this car accident. She knows about it. But I didn't go into all the gory details with her and tell her how it affected me. Whereas, my adoptive mother and I phone back and forth every week. She knows all the legalities. All the medical stuff. She's been there to help me and the kids. She's gone through a lot with me. That's why I say we are very close. She's always been there for me. She's my mother. We have a very close relationship. It may not be biological but she's my mother' (female, age 35).

Contact with the birth mother had given these adoptees a stronger sense of self as the adoptive parents' child. The adoptive parents had attended such major life-change events of the adoptees' first step, school entrance, graduation, marriage, and childbirth. These parents were present during the adoptees' times of joy and sadness. They had supported the adoptees' failures and successes. These adoptees turned, therefore, to their adoptive parents as a major support for the effects of contact with their birth mothers.

Adoptees who had told their adoptive parents about their search found this process much easier than adoptees who maintained closed, pretence, or suspicion awareness contexts in their adoptive parent–child interactions. 'Open' adoptees discussed the outcome of their contact and its effects directly with their adoptive parents. These discussions relieved the adoptive parents' fears about contact at the same time as it helped the adoptees come to terms with the results of their search. This process of sharing the search and contact experience strengthened their adoptive parent–child bonds and entrenched the adoptive parents' role as the primary parental figures in the adoptee's life.

Adoptees who did not discuss their search and contact experience with their adoptive parents expressed their sense of appreciation for adoption and strengthened their adoptive parent–child relationship in other ways. They increased their visits to their adoptive parents' home, telephoned more regularly, and made it a point to share holiday times or special events with their adoptive families. However, the process of searching for and contacting their birth mother had not altered their view of their adoptive parents' possible reaction to those activities. Like the following adoptee, they claimed that 'I can't tell them because I really believe that they would be hurt by it. If it came up, I might even lie. Because I really do feel it would hurt them. Especially, my dad. He is not in great health. And they might overreact. Because that's the type they are. They might even cut me off. Like, they still worry about me if they call and I'm not home. They would always think that I was at her place or something. It's not worth it' (female, age 30).

Those adoptees who maintained contact with their birth mothers experienced more stress from their decision not to tell their adoptive parents about their search than did 'rejected,' 'disengaged,' or 'rejecting' adoptees. Trying to maintain 'open' birth mother contact and keep it a secret from their adoptive parents created stress for both relationships. For this reason, some adoptees decided to disclose their search to their adoptive parents after they achieved an adoptee–birth mother relationship. Others continued to use pretence awareness contexts. For example, some introduced the birth mother to their children as a 'friend from work' in fear that the children would mention her in front of the adoptive parents. Others fabricated stories about appointments with or phone calls from a 'friend' who was, in reality, the birth mother. Thus, the woman quoted above claimed 'open' contact with her birth mother but experienced her adoptive parent–child interactions within a pretence awareness context. Yet when she took such action, she altered her 'open' birth mother contact into a 'pretence' relationship. This adoptee described her situation:

'She phoned me at home on the day of my wedding. Of course, she couldn't come. They weren't invited. They came to the church and watched the ceremony and then left. But, she phoned me that morning. My mom was in the kitchen. So, I couldn't say anything. She said, "I just want to tell you that I love you." I thought that was so nice. But, I couldn't say anything back.

And, we were all here a couple of summers ago. My mom and dad called and asked what we were doing. I panicked because I thought they might be coming up. What was I going to say? And my birth mother and her husband bought us a nice wedding present. My mom wanted to know who I got it from. My husband and I had planned the same story, in case, she asked. Then, when my daughter was born, they wanted to know who got me certain presents. You've always got to have an answer. (Female, age 30)

Such contact situations demonstrate how non-disclosure permeates the adoptive parent–child and, the adoptee–birth parent interaction process. Contact with the birth mother had opened the awareness context surrounding the adoptees' genealogical background and the events of their conception, birth, and relinquishment. These particular adoptees believed, however, that their adoptive parents' could not accept their search and contact activities. They became involved, therefore, in elaborate schemes to try to maintain and protect these two, significant relationships. The demand for secrecy created further secrecy (Haimes and Timms, 1985: 100). In fact, those who introduced the birth mother as a 'friend' to their children have transferred that secrecy to the next generation.

CONTACT WITH THE BIRTH MOTHER AS A LIFE-CHANGE EVENT

Andrews (1979: 59) has suggested that the search for and contact with the birth mother reflects 'one of the many searches for meaning that all people must take as they proceed through the life cycle.' Adoptees contemplate their genetic and genealogical background in the same way as others contemplate different parts of self during various periods of introspection. The special circumstances of adoption and the demands of non-disclosure emphasize that process by keeping certain parts of self hidden from adoptees. Those adoptees who desire a better understanding of self seek contact with their birth mother as a way to obtain access to those hidden parts.

Before the search for and contact with the birth mother, the adoptees in this study organized their social world around the constraints of non-disclosure. They maintained an image of self as adopted persons raised within an adoptive family structure. When they gained access to their genetic and genealogical background, they placed themselves within a biosocial context that was consistent with this image. They disregarded the birth mother's biological claim on them by placing their adoptive parents in the position of 'real' parents. They resisted the effects of an undesirable outcome of contact by referring to their separate experiences within the adoptive family structure. They incorporated their genetic and genealogical background as early biographical data that helped explain their individuality. The search for and contact with the birth mother presented little threat, therefore, to their self-concept as adoptees or to the organization of their social world.

Over time, these adoptees perceived their search and contact experience as merely another life-change event that had passed for them. For example, one woman remarked, 'I really need to go through this folder on my search and remind myself of the events. Because, you forget. For the most part of my life, I don't think about it. This folder hasn't been out of the cupboard for months. I had to dust it to bring it to you. Because, I'm busy. I'm a professional woman and I have a family and my hobbies. So, I don't have time to sit around and think about it. I don't think that most adoptees do. It's just part of me now. Like, my adoption' (female, age 44). This factor is true, also, for 'open' contact adoptees who must integrate their adoptee–birth mother relationship as a part of their social world. As one of them stated, 'we keep in touch regularly. But mostly I'm busy. My job is shift work. And the kids. And my husband. They have an active social life themselves. Mostly, I don't really think about it. She's there' (female, age 31).

In this way, like other life-change events, the search and contact with the birth mother became a part of the adoptees' biography. However, because of the special circumstances of this life-change event, it was placed within context of their early biographical history as adoptees. Thus, one man remarked, 'I never volunteered the information that I was adopted unless I was asked directly. I didn't want to be thought of as different from the rest. But now I know. Before, you didn't want to explain your situation because you didn't have the information to explain it. It's easier now. I'm quite comfortable with it. It's like coming out of the closet' (male, age 35).

The adoptees in this study claimed unsatisfactory presentations of self because their biographical discontinuities prevented them from offering adequate information about their genealogical and genetic past to those in their present. At such times, their attempt to explain themselves required a revelation of their adoptive status and an accompanying discreditation as a person with a social stigma. Because these adoptees could not determine when others' demands for this background information might arise, they lacked power to determine the flow of social interaction. Their search became an attempt, therefore, to normalize self and neutralize the social stigma conveyed by their adoption.

By providing access to the information banned by non-disclosure, search for and contact with the birth mother offered these adoptees a practical way to resolve their biographical discontinuities. They managed the interaction process more effectively with this background material and perceived their presentations of self in a more satisfactory manner. Thus, despite the findings of their search or the outcome of their contact, they expressed satisfaction with their search and contact experience. The level of satisfaction expressed depended upon the extent of genealogical background information acquired rather than the type of adoptee–birth mother contact obtained. For this reason, 'rejected,' 'rejecting,' and 'disengaged' adoptees might declare more satisfaction with contact outcome than an 'open contact' adoptee who found a birth mother unwilling to disclose the identity of the birth father or details on the adoptee's conception, birth, and relinquishment.

A major consequence of search is the clarification of the adoptive parents' dominant position in the adoptee's life. Contact with the birth mother destroys that part of the motherhood myth that claims the primacy of the biological blood bond. When these adoptees confronted the reality of a 'stranger' who they had to get to know, they recognized the fallacy of this myth. Those adoptees who maintained contact with their birth mother cultivated their adoptee–birth mother relationship by using their common blood bond as an interactional base and forming a mutual history of shared interaction that began on the day of their first contact. In contrast, the continuity of experience in the adoptive parent–child relationship emphasized the strength of their adoptive parent–child bonds. In this way, contact with the birth mother increased the adoptees' appreciation for their adoptive backgrounds and solidified their perception of self as an 'adoptee.' By placing their biological background information within the context of their early biography and merging it as part of their adoptive identity, search and contact became an adjunct of their adoptive history. It occupied a place in their biography as one more life-change event that presented them with a greater self-understanding and a stronger acceptance of their lives.

8

Conclusion

Non-disclosure poses a dilemma for adoptees raised in a society in which biological kinship governs. Many adoptees question their sense of self because they lack the genetic and genealogical information carried by those ties. Large numbers of adoptees have tried to resolve this sense of uncertainty about self through a search for and contact with their birth mother. The success of their search activities has encouraged a strong public movement for the release of identifying information to all members of the adoption triad–adoptees, birth parents, and adoptive parents. Little change has been effected by these groups, however. Generations of adoptees are being raised, still, without full knowledge of their biological backgrounds. The public's concern over the negative consequences of contact with the birth mother keeps secrecy entrenched firmly in the adoption contract.

Non-disclosure was instituted in adoption, originally, as a protection for all three members of the adoption triad. It safeguarded the adoptive parents' position as the custodial parents, insulated birth parents from the public humiliation of a birth out of wedlock, and sheltered adoptees from an emotional confrontation with birth parents who had relinquished them. Few predicted the problems that non-disclosure produced for adopted children who questioned their genealogical and genetic background or the events surrounding their conception, birth, and relinquishment. Few considered the meaning of this information for the adoptees' perception of self or for the social construction of identity in modern Western society.

The continued rise in the number of searching adoptees has been met with a growing body of research literature on the adopted population's need for contact with the birth mother. Those research studies reveal the adoptees' desire for contact as a need to 'fill in' the identity 'gaps' produced through non-disclosure. By restricting adoptees' knowledge of their biological background and the events surrounding their conception, birth, and relinquishment, non-disclosure hides certain parts of self from them. In contrast, reunited adoptees gain a sense of personal cohesion and inner serenity from the genealogical and genetic knowledge revealed through the search for and contact with the birth mother. In this way, the social processes involved in this search and contact respond to the institutional failings of an adoption process based on secrecy.

This book builds on that research literature through its analysis of the effects of non-disclosure on the adoptees' presentation of self. The adoptees in this study believed they had been stigmatized socially through adoption. In their accounts of this stigmatization process, these adoptees described how the institutional requirement of non-disclosure created biographical discontinuities that intruded upon the process of social interaction. At such times, to save their self-presentations, they had to acknowledge their adoptive status and reveal their social stigma to others. Because these adoptees could not predict when such social situations might arise, they could not manage their stigma trait effectively. They felt powerless over the social interaction process and helpless over their ability to achieve a satisfactory presentation of self.

An examination of the social processes involved in the search for and contact with the birth mother requires a theoretical perspective that considers both the individual and his or her society. The symbolic interactionist theoretical approach views social life as a continually negotiated process taking place among individuals. From this perspective, the meanings of objects (for example, self and identity) emerge from the actions taken by others towards those objects. Furthermore, because humans are self-reflective they create identities that manifest the actions taken towards them. They produce social worlds or universes of discourse from their social experiences with others. Individuals are active participants in, rather than passive recipients of, their society.

The interactionist concepts of self, personal identity, reflected appraisals of others, motive talk, and social interaction present the search for and contact with the birth mother as dynamic, social processes involving several actors. These theoretical concepts presume neither an ideal type of search nor outcome of contact. Instead, the social processes of the search for and contact with the birth mother depend greatly upon the perceptions of the particular interactants involved. Some adoptees may want only medical background information. Some may desire long-term, open, mother–child contact relationships. Some may never search, but prefer the status quo. The adoptee's choice depends greatly upon the meaning that this background information holds for him or her and the organization of his or her social world.

This view of the effects of non-disclosure takes the focus of search away from individual adoptees and places it within the larger social context of which they are a part. From this position, the desire for contact with the birth mother is seen, no longer, as a product of a dysfunctional identity structure, poor adoptive parent–child bonding, or unsatisfactory outcome of adoption. This view interprets the desire for such a search as merely one of many possible responses to the demands of non-disclosure. If adoptees seek contact with their birth mother in an attempt to counterbalance their social stigma, then, interest in the search may vary according to the relevance of this missing background material for a satisfactory presentation of self. From this perspective, one can easily explain the diversity of searchers, search expectations, and contact responses found in the research literature. That diversity represents the wide variety of individuals involved in adoption and the vast range of social circumstances that may raise the desire of adoptees for more complete genealogical and genetic backgrounds.

In their attempt to understand, fully, the social worlds from the perspective of the individuals involved in them, interactionists apply an eclectic methodological approach to their research studies. The data analysis in this book is based on that type of approach. I conducted participant-observation sessions at Parent Finders meetings and and followed these by intensive, open-ended, semi-structured interview schedules with a randomly selected sample of sixty reunited adoptees. The accounts presented in those interview schedules were compared continually with the participant observation findings. Comparisons were made, as well, with the findings of the search and contact research literature, media reports, and biographical publications of personal search and contact experiences. This method presents multiple views that validate the accounts given by the sixty adoptees who appear in this book.

These sixty adoptees represent the full range of adoptees found in other search and contact studies. Like the majority of searchers, they experienced doubts about their identity as adoptees raised within adoptive family structures. Those doubts emerged from others' curiosity over their biological background and their 'real' identity as biological children who had been relinquished. In response to those social interactions these adoptees developed a latent desire for contact with the birth mother as a way to access their hidden parts of self and establish a coherent identity. It was not until a major life-change event brought this latent desire for contact to the attention of significant others that these adoptees took serious search action. With this social support, they broke the constraints of their society and initiated a search that led to contact with the birth mother.

These adoptees described a series of search stages in which adoptees gather, and sort through, bits and pieces of their genealogical background that lead to the identity of the birth mother. Those stages include (1) contact with a search agency, (2) gaining access to the birth mother's surname, (3) confronting a birth identity, (4) getting non-identifying information, (5) obsession with the search, and (6) identification of the birth mother. Each stage involves access to background material that uncovers more of the adoptees' hidden parts of self. Some adoptees may themselves discontinue the search when they gain the background material that they desire (for example, medical background information). Others may become so obsessed with the search that they stop only when they identify the birth mother's current address. Although a general pattern of search exists, each search process is a singular experience for those individuals who confront the institutional barriers of non-disclosure. The adoptees in this study exemplify those adoptees who continued the search process to its completion, that is, verification of the identity of the birth mother.

Verification of the identity of the birth mother transforms the adoptees' fantasy image into a physical reality. Once adoptees have identified the birth mother, they must decide, therefore, if they will initiate contact. Once contacted, the birth mother becomes an active participant in the contact process with an agenda of her own. These adoptees described three main types of contact based on the birth mother's attitude towards contact and her actions towards them: (1) discontinuation of contact by the birth mother, (2) discontinuation of contact by the adoptee, and (3) continued contact.

Those adoptees who established contact with the birth mother entered a process of role negotiation in which each party mediated their desires of the adoptee–birth mother contact. That role negotiation process was influenced greatly by the adoptees' perception of the birth mother's power to accept or reject their contact. For this reason, 'rejected' or 'disengaged' adoptees did not ask the birth mother for an account of her contact behaviour. To protect self from the emotional hurt produced by a possible 'second rejection,' these adoptees assigned their own explanation to their birth mother's response to contact. Those explanations reflected the adoptees' perception of the birth mother's position in the adoption triad and her overwhelming need for confidentiality concerning her status as a birth mother.

These explanations demonstrate how the vocabulary of motives used to support the institutional value of non-disclosure affect the individual experience of the search for and contact with the birth mother. Secrecy in adoption is viewed as a protection of the positions held by each member in the adoption triad. Those protections centre around three major themes: (1) concern for the primacy of the adoptive parent–child relationship, (2) concern over a possible intrusion into the birth mother's life, and (3) fear of a second rejection. Because these adoptees had internalized these three themes, they could abstract them and use them as explanations of their own search and contact experiences. Thus, 'rejected' and 'disengaged' adoptees had an acceptable explanation for the behaviour of the birth mother (such as the need for privacy) that distanced them from the effects of a possible second rejection. In a similar fashion, 'rejecting' adoptees explained their withdrawal from problematic contact with the birth mother by referring to the primacy of their adoptive parent–child relationship. These adoptees could also disclaim a sense of connection with the birth mother's character or lifestyle because their adoptive family experience had neutralized the effects of their common biological tie.

Face-to-face contact reinforces the adoptees' sense of disconnection from the birth mother. When the adoptees in this study met a 'stranger' instead of a birth 'mother,' they appreciated more fully the gap of time and social experience produced by adoption. Consequently, those adoptees involved in adoptee–birth mother relationships needed some other basis for continued contact. Their ability to find another basis for contact affected the type of adoptee–birth mother contact established. 'Friends' and 'parent–child' interactions were more enjoyable than 'duty' because adoptee and birth mother had found other ways to interact that did not focus on relinquishment. In this way, both interactants could relax as the 'gap' of time and social experience since relinquishment was slowly closed by new social encounters upon which a mutual relationship could be based.

Glaser and Strauss's (1967b: 430) awareness context paradigm presents an additional understanding of the effects of non-disclosure. Secrecy surrounds the members of the adoption triad within a closed awareness context. That closed awareness context produces uncertainty for all members of the adoption triad when interactions involving these particular status positions arise. At such times, adoptees, birth parents, and adoptive parents experience doubt about others' identity as well as their own identity in the eyes of others (Glaser and Strauss, 1967b: 430). Each member of the adoption triad expresses those doubts in a way that reflects their position in that triad. Thus, adoptive parents experience doubt over their identity as the adoptees' real parents, birth mothers experience uncertainty about their morality as women who relinquished their children, and adoptees experience uncertainty over whether they are a product of their biological background or their adoptive experience.

This study concentrates on the effects of this closed awareness context for searching adoptees. That analysis also provides considerable insight into the impact of secrecy on the other two members of the adoption triad. For example, adoptive parents may not be able to hide their fear of a possible intrusion by the birth mother when they discuss adoption with their adopted children. In response to this perceived fear, many adoptees conceal their search activities from their parents or pretend no interest in contact with their birth mothers. When these adoptees take such action, they perpetuate the secrecy inherent in the adoption contract. They demonstrate, also, how the three themes used to support non-disclosure permeate the interactional context when the topic of adoption arises.

In contrast, the search for and contact with the birth mother creates an open awareness context for adoptees who learn about their biological backgrounds and the events of their conception, birth, and relinquishment. The extent of openness depends, however, upon the birth mother's ability or willingness to provide such information. In this study, rejected adoptees reported the least openness because the birth mother severed contact immediately without providing further background information. Adoptees who found the birth mother deceased experienced a similar reaction. Many other adoptees engaged, however, in pretence or suspicion awareness contexts with the birth mother because she would not respond adequately to their questions. The power given to the birth mother to either accept or deny contact placed these adoptees in a vulnerable position of negotiation in the flow, direction, and content of their adoptee–birth mother interactions.

Knowledge of the identity of the birth father had a direct effect on the process of interaction established between birth mothers and adoptees. The adoptees' main objective of search was discovery of hidden parts of self. The birth mother represented only one-half of that missing background information. Once these adoptees had learned about the birth mother, they wanted more information on the birth father. The birth mother's willingness to supply such information had a major impact on her own adoptee–birth mother interactions. If she created an open awareness context in those interactions by discussing the birth father's identity, she communicated a respect for her birth child's full identity as an adopted person. If she refused to be open and surrounded her adoptee–birth mother interactions within pretence, suspicion, or closed awareness contexts, she reinforced her birth child's powerless position as an adopted person suffering from the demands of non-disclosure. Because these adoptees interpreted the birth mother's actions as a symbol of her concern for them, they viewed her refusal to be open as a rejection of their personal needs and a reflection of her status as an uncaring birth mother.

In such ways, the examination of the search for and contact with the birth mother exemplifies the importance of the reflected appraisals of others for the emergence of self and identity. These adoptees perceived unsatisfactory presentations of self when their biographical discontinuities intruded upon the process of social interaction. They could not resist unwanted identity imputations from others because they were unclear, themselves, about those hidden parts of self. Because they lacked the ability to control the release of their background information to others, and thereby dispute or combat others' discrimination against them, they felt 'flawed,' 'incomplete,' 'disjointed,' and 'deficient.' In this way, others' reflected appraisals undermined adoptees' personal identity and contributed to their social stigma. This was the main motivation for the search. The adoptees in this study believed their genetic and genealogical information would make their identities more credible.

Contact with the birth mother helped these adoptees achieve their search objective. It provided them with the genealogical data needed to combat the unwanted identity imputations attributed to their adoptive status. For the first time in their lives, these adoptees possessed the power to convey and control the release of this type of information about self. Because they perceived that this information satisfied others' curiosity, they experienced greater satisfaction with their presentations of self and more certainty about such interactions. Their sense of acceptance by others helps to explain the new sense of self-composure and personal security reported after the search ends.

Viewed from this perspective, the reports of satisfaction with the outcome of contact are understandable. These adoptees had fulfilled their original search goal. They had neutralized the effects of secrecy in adoption. However, the extent of their biological knowledge moderated that level of satisfaction. Because adoptees who received considerable genealogical and genetic information removed more biological discontinuities, those adoptees experienced more satisfaction than adoptees who discovered their birth mother deceased or adoptees who could not trust the birth mother's reports. Satisfaction with contact with the birth mother is a multidimensional measure that calls for deeper consideration of the assessment of the adoptees' search for and the outcome of the contact with the birth mother than has been considered previously in the research literature.

Yet, the search for and contact with the birth mother do not eliminate the social stigma of adoption. These social processes present adoptees with merely another way to manage their stigma trait. What contact with the birth mother does offer is a new social relationship for which the members of the adoption triad and their society have not prepared fully. As more and more adoptees seek contact with birth mothers and birth fathers, more and more families will be affected by the introduction of a 'stranger' who wishes to be accepted and take his or her 'rightful' position in that family structure. Whether that 'stranger' is a birth parent, an adoptee, a birth sibling, or an adoptive parent, more research is needed on how this new family dynamic unfolds. In particular, there is need for more study on the other family members' perceptions of these social processes. The experiences reported by the adoptees in this book merely offer a prototype upon which such research may develop.

References

Alexander, C. Norman, Jr., and Mary Glenn Wiley. 1981. 'Situated Activity and Identity Formation,' in M. Rosenberg and R.A. Turner (eds.), *Social Psychology: Sociological Perspectives*. New York: Basic Books 269–89.

Anderson, Robert S. 1989. 'The Nature of Adoptee Search: Adventure, Cure, or Growth?' *Child Welfare* 68: 623–32.

Andrews, Roberta. 1979. 'A Clinical Appraisal of Searching.' *Public Welfare* 37: 15–21.

Aumend, Sue A., and Marjie C. Barrett. 1984. 'Self-Concept and Attitudes toward Adoption: A Comparison of Searching and Nonsearching Adoptees.' *Child Welfare* 63: 251–59.

Babbie, Earl. 1992. *The Practice of Social Research*. Belmont: Calif.: Wadsworth.

Barnes, J.A. 1963. 'Some Ethical Problems in Modern Field Work.' *British Journal of Sociology* 14: 118–34.

Becker, Howard. 1970. 'Personal Change in Adult Life,' in Gregory P. Stone and Harvey A. Farberman (eds.), *Social Psychology through Symbolic Interaction*. Waltham, Mass.: Ginn-Blaisdell, 583–93.

Becker, Howard, and Blanche Geer. 1957. 'Participant Observation and Interviewing: A Comparison.' *Human Organization* 16: 28–32.

Benet, Mary Katherine. 1976. *The Character of Adoption*. London: Cape.

Berger, Peter, and Thomas Luckman. 1967. *The Social Construction of Reality*. New York: Doubleday.

Blalock, H.M. 1960. *Social Statistics*. New York: McGraw-Hill.

Blumer, Herbert. 1969. *Symbolic Interactionism: Perspective and Method*. Englewood Cliffs, NJ: Prentice-Hall.

Braden, J. 1970. 'Adoption in a Changing World.' *Social Casework* 5: 486.

Campbell, L. 1979. 'The Birthparents' Right to Know.' *Public Welfare* 37: 22–7.

Caplan, Paula J. 1989. *Don't Blame Mother*. New York: Harper and Row.

Charon, Joel M. 1992. *Symbolic Interactionism: An Introduction, an Interpretation, an Integration*. Englewood Cliffs, NJ: Prentice-Hall.

Chodorow, Nancy. 1978. *The Reproduction of Mothering: Psychoanalysis and the Sociology of Gender*. Los Angeles: University of California Press.

Clothier, F. 1943. 'The Psychology of the Adopted Child.' *Mental Hygiene* 27: 222–30.

Cooley, Charles Horton. 1902. *Human Nature and the Social Order*. New York: Scribner's.

Dally, A. 1982. *Inventing Motherhood; The Consequences of an Ideal*. London: Burnett Books.

Davenport, Joan. 1984. *Years of Caring*. Children's Aid Society of Hamilton-Wentworth.

Day, Cyril. 1979. 'Access to Birth Records: General Register Office Study.' *Adoption and Fostering* 98: 17–28.

Depp, Carol Hope. 1982. 'After Reunion: Perceptions of Adult Adoptees, Adoptive Parents, and Birth Parents.' *Child Welfare* 61: 115–19.

Deutsch, Morton, and Robert M. Krauss. 1965. *Theories in Social Psychology*. New York: Basic Books.

Douglas, Jack D. 1976. *Investigative Social Research: Individual and Team Field Research*. Beverly Hills: Sage.

Duffy, Ann, and Norene Pupo. 1992. *Part-Time Paradox: Connecting Gender, Work and Family*. Toronto: McClelland and Stewart.

Duffy, Ann, Nancy Mandell, and Norene Pupo. 1989. *Few Choices: Women, Work, and Family*. Toronto: Garamond Press.

Dukette, R. 1962. 'Discussion of Thoughts Regarding the Etiology of Psychological Differences in Adopted Children.' *Child Welfare* 41: 66–71.

Eichler, Margrit. 1988. *Families in Canada Today*, 2nd ed. Toronto: Gage.

Erickson, Kai. 1965. 'A Comment on Disguised Observation in Sociology.' *Social Problems* 14: 366–73.

Fiegleman, W., and A.R. Silverman. 1979. 'Preferential Adoption: A New Mode of Family Formation.' *Social Casework* 14: 296–305.

– 1983. *Chosen Children: New Patterns of Adoption Relationships*. New York: Prager.

Festinger, Leon, and Daniel Katz. 1953. *Research Methods in the Behavioral Sciences*. New York: Holt, Rinehart, and Winston.

Fisher, Florence. 1973. *The Search for Anna Fisher*. New York: Arthus Fields.

Flynn, L. 1979. 'Adoption: A Parent's Perspective.' *Public Welfare* 37: 34–7.

Fox, Bonnie J. 1993. *Family Patterns, Gender Relations*. Toronto: Oxford University Press.

Garber, Ralph. 1985. *Disclosure of Adoption Information*. Report of the Special Commissioner to the Honourable John Sweeney, Minister of Community and Social Services, Government of Ontario.

Geidman, Judith S., and Linda P. Brown. 1989. *Birth Bond: Reunions between Birthparents and Adoptees*. Far Hill, NJ: New Horizons Press.

Glaser, Barney G., and Anselm L. Strauss. 1965. *Awareness of Dying*. Chicago: Aldine.

– 1967a. *The Discovery of Grounded Theory: Strategies for Qualitative Research*. New York: Aldine.

– 1967b. 'Awareness Contexts and Social Interaction,' in J.G. Manis and B.N. Meltzer (eds.), *Symbolic Interaction*. Boston: Allyn and Bacon, 429–47.

Gochros, H. 1967. 'A Study of Caseworker–Adoptive Parent Relationship in Postplacement Service.' *Child Welfare* 46: 317–25.

Goffman, Erving. 1959. *The Presentation of Self in Everyday Life*. New York: Doubleday.

– 1963. *Stigma: Notes on the Management of Spoiled Identity*. Englewood Cliffs, NJ: Prentice-Hall.

Gonyo, Barbara, and Kenneth W. Watson. 1988. 'Searching in Adoption.' *Public Welfare* 46: 14–22.

Griffith, Keith C. 1991. *The Right to Know Who You Are*. Ottawa: Katherine W. Kimbell.

Haas, Jack, and William Shaffir. 1978. *Shaping Identity in Canadian Society*. Scarborough, Ont.: Prentice-Hall.

– 1980. 'Fieldworkers' Mistakes at Work: Problems in Maintaining Research and Research Bargains,' in W.B. Shaffir, R.A. Stebbins, and A. Turowetz (eds.), *Fieldwork Experience: Qualitative Approaches to Social Research*. New York: St Martin's Press, 244–255.

Haimes, Erica, and Noel Trimms. 1985. *Adoption, Identity, and Social Policy: The Search for Distant Relatives*. London: Bower.

Harrington, J.D. 1979. 'Legislative Reform Moves Slowly.' *Public Welfare* 37: 49–59.

– 1980. 'The Courts Contend with Sealed Adoption Records.' *Public Welfare* 38: 12–15.

Hepworth, H. Philip. 1980. *Foster Care and Adoption in Canada*. Ottawa: Canadian Council on Social Development.

Hewitt, J.P. 1979. *Self and Society: Symbolic Interactionist Social Psychology*. Boston: Allyn and Bacon.

Inglis, Kate. 1984. *Living Mistakes*. Australia: George Allen Unwin.

Jaffee, B., and D. Fanshel. 1970. *How They Fared in Adoption*. New York: Columbia University Press.

Kadushin, A. 1966. 'Adoptive Parenthood: A Hazardous Adventure?' *Social Work* 11: 30–9.

Kadushin, A., and F. Seidl. 1971. 'Adoption Failure.' *Social Work* 16: 32–8.

Kirby, Sandra, and McKenna, Kate. 1989. *Experience, Research, Social Change: Methods from the Margins.* Toronto: Garamond Press.

Kirk, David H. 1959. 'A Dilemma of Adoption Parenthood: Incongruous Role Obligations.' *Marriage and Family Living* 21: 316–26.

- 1964. *Shared Fate: A Theory of Adoption and Mental Health.* Toronto: Collier-Macmillan.

- 1981. *Adoptive Kinship: A Modern Institution in Need of Reform.* Toronto: Butterworths.

Krugman, Dorothy. 1964. 'Reality in Adoption.' *Child Welfare* 43: 349–58.

Kubler-Ross, Elizabeth. 1970. *On Death and Dying.* New York: Macmillan.

Lauer, R.H., and W.H. Handel. 1977. *Social Psychology: The Theory and Application of Symbolic Interactionism.* Boston: Houghton Mifflin.

Lemon, Ruth. 1959.'Rear View Mirror: An Experience with Completed Adoptions.' *The Social Worker,* 27: 41–51.

Levine, H., and A. Estable. 1990. *The Politics of Motherhood: A Feminist Critique of Theory and Practice.* Ottawa: Centre for Social Welfare Studies.

Lifton, Betty Jean. 1979. *Lost and Found: The Adoption Experience.* New York: Dial Press.

Lofland, John. 1971. *Analyzing Social Settings.* Belmont, Calif.: Wadsworth.

Luxton, Meg. 1980. *More Than a Labour of Love.* Toronto: Women's Press.

March, Karen. 1990. 'The Stranger Who Bore Me: Adoptee–Birth Mother Interactions.' PhD Dissertation, Department of Sociology, McMaster University, Hamilton, Ontario.

Marcus, Claire. 1981. *Who Is My Mother?* Toronto: Macmillan.

McCall, George J., and J.L. Simmons. 1968. *Identities and Interactions.* New York: Free Press.

McKuen, Rod. 1978. *Finding My Father: One Man's Search for Identity.* New York: Free Press.

McNamara, Joan. 1975. *The Adoption Advisor.* New York: Hawthorne Books.

McWhinnie, A.M. 1967. *Adopted Children: How They Grow Up.* Routledge and Kegan Paul.

Mead, George Herbert. 1934. *Mind, Self, and Society.* Chicago: University of Chicago Press.

Meltzer, Bernard N., John W. Petras, and Larry T. Reynolds. 1975. *Symbolic Interactionism: Genesis, Varieties, and Criticism.* Boston: Routledge and Kegan Paul.

Miall, Charlene. 1986. 'The Stigma of Involuntary Childlessness.' *Social Problems* 33: 268–82.

- 1987. 'The Stigma of Adoptive Parent Status: Perceptions of Community Attitudes toward Adoption and the Experience of Informal Sanctioning.' *Family Relations* 36: 34–9.

Mills, C. Wright. 1940. 'Situated Actions and Vocabularies of Motives.' *American Journal of Sociology* 5: 904–13.

Nett, Emily M. 1993. *Canadian Families: Past and Present*, 2nd ed. Toronto: Butterworths.

Neuman, W. Lawrence. 1994. *Social Research Methods: Qualitative and Quantitative Approaches*, 2nd ed. Massachusetts: Allyn and Bacon.

Norvell, Melissa, and Rebecca Guy. 1977. 'A Comparison of Self-Concept in Adopted and Non-Adopted Adolescents.' *Adolescence* 12: 24–35.

Ontario. Ministry of Community and Social Services. 1990. *Adoption Disclosure Registry*. Toronto: Government of Ontario.

Pacheco, Frances, and Robert Eme. 1993. 'An Outcome Study of Reunion between Adoptees and Biological Parents.' *Child Welfare* 72: 53–64.

Paton, Jean. 1954. *The Adopted Break Silence*. Philadelphia: Life History Study Centre.

Prus, Robert. 1987. 'Generic Social Processes: Maximizing Conceptual Development in Ethnographic Research.' *Journal of Contemporary Ethnography* 16: 250–93.

Redmond, Wendy, and Sherry Sleightholm. 1982. *Once Removed: Voices from Inside the Adoption Triangle*. Toronto: McGraw-Hill Ryerson.

Rich, Adrienne. 1986. *Of Woman Born: Motherhood as Experience and Institution*, 10th ed. New York: Norton.

Ripple, Lillian. 1968. 'A Follow-up Study of Adopted Children.' *Social Service Review* 42: 479–99.

Rosenberg, Morris. 1981. 'The Self-Concept: Social Product and Social Force,' in Morris Rosenberg and Ralph H. Turner (eds.), *Social Psychology: Sociological Perspectives*. New York: Basic Books.

Rosenzweig-Smith, J. 1988. 'Factors Associated with Successful Reunions of Adult Adoptees and Biological Parents.' *Child Welfare* 67: 411–22.

Roth, Julius. 1960. 'Comments on Secret Observation.' *Social Problems* 9: 283–4.

Rossiter, Amy. 1988. *From Private to Public: A Feminist Exploration in Early Mothering*. Toronto: Woman's Press.

Sachdev, Paul. 1989. *Unlocking the Adoption Files*. Toronto: Lexington Books.

– 1992. 'Adoption Reunion and After: A Study of the Search Process and Experience of Adoptees.' *Child Welfare* 71: 53–67.

Sants, H.J. 1965. 'Genealogical Bewilderment in Children with Substitute Parents.' *British Journal of Medical Psychology* 37: 133–41.

Schechter, M.D. 1960. 'Observations on Adopted Children.' *Archives of General Psychiatry* 3: 21–32.

Schechter, M.D., P.V. Carlson, J.Q. Simmons, and H.H. Work. 1964. 'Emotional Problems in the Adoptee.' *Archives of General Psychiatry* 10: 37–46.

Schur, E.M. 1983. *Labelling Women Deviant: Gender, Stigma, and Social Control.* Philadelphia: Temperline Press.

Shaffir, William, Robert Stebbins, and Allan Turowetz. 1980. *Fieldwork Experience: Qualitative Approaches to Social Research.* New York: St Martin's Press.

Shibutani, Tamotsu. 1961. *Society and Personality: An Interactionist Approach to Social Psychology.* Englewood Cliffs, NJ: Prentice-Hall.

Silverman, Phyllis R., Lee Campbell, Patricia Patti, and Carolyn Briggs Style. 1988. 'Reunions between Adoptees and Birth Parents: The Birth Parents' Experience.' *Social Work* 33: 523–8.

Simpson, M., H. Timm, and H.I. McCubbin. 1981. 'Adoptees in Search of Their Past: Policy Induced Strain on Adoptive Families and Birth Parents.' *Family Relations* 30: 427–34.

Small, J.W. 1979. 'Discrimination against the Adoptee.' *Public Welfare* 37: 38–43.

Sobol, Michael, and Jean Cardiff. 1983. 'A Sociopsychological Investigation of Adult Adoptees' Search for Birth Parents.' *Family Relations* 32: 477–83.

Solinger, Rickie. 1992. *Wake Up Little Susie: Single Pregnancy and Race before Roe v. Wade.* New York: Routledge.

Sorosky, A.D., A. Baran, and R. Pannor.. 1974. 'The Reunion of Adoptees and Birth Relatives.' *Journal of Youth and Adolescence* 3: 195–206.

– 1975. 'Identity Conflicts in Adoptees.' *American Journal of Orthopsychiatry* 45: 18–27.

– 1978. *The Adoption Triangle.* New York: Anchor.

Spradley, James P. 1980. *Participant Observation.* New York: Holt, Rinehart and Winston.

Stone, Gregory P. 1962. 'Appearance and the Self,' in Arnold M. Rose (ed.), *Human Behaviour and Social Processes.* Boston: Houghton Mifflin 86–118.

Stoneman, L., C. Blakely, A. Douglas, and J. Webber. 1985. 'Post Adoption Service to Birth Parents.' Toronto: Children's Aid Society of Metropolitan Toronto.

Stoneman, L., J. Thompson, and J. Webber. 1980. 'Adoption Reunion: A Study of the Effect of Reunion upon Members of the Adoption Triad and Their Families.' Toronto: Children's Aid Society of Metropolitan Toronto.

Strauss, Anselm. 1969. *Mirrors and Masks: The Search for Identity.* San Francisco: Sociology Press.

Stryker, Sheldon. 1980. *Symbolic Interactionism.* Menlo Park, Calif.: Benjamin/Cummings.

Sweeney, John. 1986. *Ontario's New Adoption Disclosure Policy.* Toronto: Ontario Ministry of Community and Social Services.

Thomas, William I. 1931. 'The Definition of the Situation,' in Jerome G. Manis and Bernard N. Meltzer (eds.), *Symbolic Interaction: A Reader in Social Psychology.* Boston: Allyn and Bacon, 1967 reprint, 315–41.

Thompson, J. 1979. 'Roots and Rights – A Challenge for Adoption.' *Social Worker* 47: 13–15.

Thompson, J., J. Webber, A. Stoneman, and D. Harrison. 1978. 'The Adoption Rectangle: A Study of Adult Adoptees' Search for Birth Family History and Implications for Adoption Service.' Toronto: Children's Aid Society of Metropolitan Toronto.

– 1980. 'Adoption Reunion.' Toronto: Children's Aid Society of Metropolitan Toronto.

Toussieng, P.W. 1962. 'Thoughts Regarding the Etiology of Psychological Difficulties in Adopted Children.' *Public Welfare* 40: 59–65.

– 1971. 'Realizing the Potential in Adoptions.' *Child Welfare* 50: 322–7.

Triseliotis, J. 1973. *In Search of Origins*. London: Routledge and Kegan Paul.

Veevers, J.E. 1980. *Childless by Choice*. Toronto: Butterworths.

Verney, Thomas. 1981. *The Secret Life of the Unborn Child*. New York: Dell.

Wearing, Betsy. 1984. *The Ideology of Motherhood*. Australia: George Allen and Unwin.

Weinstein, E.A. 1968. 'Adoption.' *International Encyclopedia of the Social Sciences*. New York: Macmillan Free Press.

Williamson, J.B., D.A. Karp, and J.R. Dalphin. 1977. *The Research Craft*. Toronto: Little, Brown.

Zeilinger, Robert. 1979. 'The Need to Know vs. the Right to Know.' *Public Welfare* 37: 44–7.

Author Index

Subject Index